Benjamin Brawley

A SHORT HISTORY
OF THE
AMERICAN NEGRO

Fourth Revised Edition

BY

BENJAMIN BRAWLEY

DECIUS.—Here lies the east: doth not the day break here?
CASCA.—No.
CINNA.—O, pardon, sir, it doth; and yon grey lines
That fret the clouds are messengers of day.

SHAKESPEARE: *Julius Caesar*

NEW YORK
THE MACMILLAN COMPANY

DEDICATED

TO THE YOUNG AMERICANS

WITH WHOM IT HAS BEEN MY PRIVILEGE

IN THE CLASSROOM TO SEEK

THE BEAUTIFUL AND THE TRUE

PREFACE

This study of the history of the American Negro endeavors simply to set forth the main facts that one might wish to know about the subject, and to supply the background for much that is read today in newspapers and magazines. The book presupposes only an elementary knowledge of American history, but it does presuppose so much. From the nature of the discussion, the treatment could hardly be primarily original, and frequent citation is made to the conclusions of investigators along special lines. At the same time, it is hoped that in more than one instance the presentation will be found to be substantially new.

The book appeared in its first form in 1913. Since then notable changes have taken place in the life of the Negro people of the United States. Now after twenty-five years, for the fourth revised edition, The Macmillan Company has given me the privilege of rewriting the work from the beginning. I hardly need to say that it is an opportunity for which I am deeply grateful. Once more, too, am I reminded of the sense of co-operation that has come to me from teachers who have found the book useful as a text. I now wish them all joy as they further pursue their task of directing Negro youth to a knowledge of their priceless heritage.

The list of *Questions for Review* at the end of the book has been one of the features of the last two editions. It is hoped that it may prove of service.

BENJAMIN BRAWLEY

Washington, D. C.
January 2, 1939

CONTENTS

CONTENTS

CHAPTER I

THE NEGRO IN THE COLONIAL PERIOD

1. **The Word** *Negro.* The word *Negro* is the Spanish and Portuguese form of the Latin adjective *niger,* meaning black. As commonly used, it is made to apply to any and all of the black and dark brown races of Africa. Such usage is not strictly correct, the term having both a narrower and a wider significance than this would imply. In Africa the real Negroes occupy only a comparatively small part of the continent, while beyond, on the islands of the Pacific Ocean, there is a branch of the Nigritian race of people only less important than the group of Negroes on the mainland.

2. **The African Slave Coast.** The Africans who came to America as slaves were by no means all of exactly the same racial stock or language group. Plantations frequently exhibited a variety of customs, for traditional enemies sometimes became brothers in servitude. The center of the colonial slave trade was the African coast extending about two hundred miles east of the Niger River. From this comparatively small region came as many slaves as from all the rest of Africa together. A number of those who came were of entirely different racial stock from the Negroes; some were Moors, and a very few were Malays from Madagascar. Such wide differences in race and tribal origin account for the marked

differences in form and feature later observed among Americans of unmixed African descent.

3. The Negro in Spanish Exploration. Negroes are mentioned in the accounts of the very early explorers of America. After 1501 they frequently appeared in the West Indies, and in 1513 thirty of them assisted Balboa in building the first ships made on the Pacific coast of America. Soon after his accession to the Spanish throne in 1516, Charles V granted license for the introduction into America of Negroes to the number of four hundred, and thereafter the importation of Negroes into the West Indies became a thriving industry. Those who came in these early years were sometimes men of considerable intelligence, who had been trained as Mohammedans or Catholics.

It was about 1525 that Negroes were first introduced within the present limits of the United States. Several were brought to a colony near what was later Jamestown, Virginia. In course of time the Negroes were so harshly treated that they rose in insurrection and fired their oppressors' houses. The settlement was broken up, and the Negroes and their Spanish companions returned to Haiti whence they had come.

The best authenticated case of Negro leadership in exploration is that of Estevanico, or Estevanillo, one of the four survivors of the ill-fated expedition of De Narvaez, who sailed from Spain on June 17, 1527. The three companions of this Negro returned to Spain, but he remained as a medicine man among the natives, and later was highly esteemed by those interested in extending the Spanish domain. To him belongs credit for the discovery of the Zuñi Indians and of New Mexico.

No part played by the Negro in these early years, however, exercised any abiding influence on the history of the race in the United States.

4. The Beginning of the African Slave Trade. The revival of slavery at the close of the Middle Ages and the beginning of the system of Negro slavery were due to the commercial expansion of Portugal in the fifteenth century. In 1441 Prince Henry sent out one, Gonzales, who captured three Moors on the African coast. These offered as ransom ten Negroes whom they had taken captive. The ten Negroes were brought to Lisbon in 1442, and two years later Prince Henry began the regular European slave trade from the Guinea coast. For fifty years his country enjoyed a monopoly of this traffic. The slaves were taken first to Europe, and then to the Spanish possessions in America, where Indian slavery had not worked well.

Spain joined in the trade in 1517, and as early as 1530 William Hawkins, an English merchant of Plymouth, visited the Guinea coast and took away a few slaves.

England really entered the field with the voyage in 1562 of Captain John Hawkins, son of William, who also went to the west coast of Africa. This seaman made two other voyages, one in 1564 in the good ship *Jesus,* and another, with Drake, in 1567, taking his slaves to the West Indies. Queen Elizabeth evidently regarded the opening of the slave trade as a worthy achievement, for when she made Hawkins a knight, she gave him for a crest the device of a Negro's head and bust with the arms securely bound in honor of this exploit.

France joined in the traffic in 1624, and then Holland, Denmark, and the American colonies followed.

5. The Development of the Slave Trade by England. The rivalry between the different countries of Europe over the slave trade soon became intense; and England, with her usual aggressiveness, assumed a commanding position. The commercial supremacy of the Dutch in the first part of the seventeenth century "excited the envy and the emulation of the English. The Navigation Ordinance of 1651 was aimed at them, and two wars were necessary to wrest the slave trade from them and place it in the hands of the English." [1] The English trade began in a large way with the granting of rights to special companies, to one in 1618, to another in 1631, and in 1662 to the Company of Royal Adventurers, which was rechartered in 1672 as the Royal African Company. James, Duke of York, later James II, was president of this last company, and it undertook to supply the West Indies with 3,000 slaves annually. In 1698, after James had been forced to leave the country and when William III was on the throne, the clamor of English merchants led to the general opening of the traffic, and by act of Parliament private traders were allowed to participate on payment of a duty of 10 per cent on English goods exported to Africa. The market for the slaves was the American colonies of the European countries, at first especially the Spanish West In-

[1] W. E. B. DuBois, *Suppression of the African Slave Trade* (Cambridge: Harvard University Press, 1896), p. 17.

dies. England regarded the slave trade as of such importance that, when she accepted the Peace of Utrecht in 1713, she insisted on having awarded to her for thirty years the exclusive right to transport slaves to the Spanish colonies in America.

6. The Planting of Slavery in the Colonies.   (a) Virginia. It is for Virginia only that we can state with definiteness the year in which Negro slaves were first brought to an English colony on the mainland. When legislation on the subject first appeared elsewhere, slaves were already present. In August, 1619, a Dutch vessel brought to Jamestown twenty Negroes, who were sold into servitude. Virginia, however, did not give statutory recognition to slavery as a system until 1661, the importations being too small to make the matter one of importance. In this year an act of the Assembly stated that Negroes were "incapable of makeing satisfaction by addition of time" [2] for the time lost in running away; and thus the institution gained a firm place in the oldest of the colonies.

(b) New England. Negroes were imported into Massachusetts from the West Indies certainly not later than 1638. In 1641 there was passed in the colony the first act on the subject of slavery, and this was the first positive act in any of the colonies with reference to the matter. The article read: "There shall never be any bond slaverie, villinage, nor captivities amongst us, unless it be lawful captives, taken in just warres, and such stran-

---

[2] William Waller Hening, *Statutes at Large, being a Collection of All the Laws of Virginia from the First Session of the Legislature, in the Year 1619* (Richmond: 1819-1820), II, 26.

gers as willingly selle themselves or are sold to us. And these shall have all the liberties and Christian usages which the law of God established in Israell concerning such persons doeth morally require. This exempts none from servitude who shall be Judged thereto by Authoritie." [3] Of the three classes of persons referred to, the first was made up of Indians, the second of white people under the system of indenture (of which more must be said), and the third of Negroes. In these early years the New England colonies were in general more concerned about Indians than about Negroes, as the presence of the former in large numbers was a constant menace while Negro slavery had not yet assumed its more serious aspects.

In Rhode Island it was enacted in 1652 that all slaves brought into the colony should be free after ten years of service. This provision was not designed, as might be supposed, to restrict slavery; it was really a step in the evolution of the system, and the limit of ten years was by no means observed. In course of time Rhode Island became a busy mart in the slave trade, being, as Dr. DuBois has said, a sort of "clearing-house for the trade of other colonies." [4]

In Connecticut there were comparatively few Negroes, and these were regarded as servants rather than as slaves, early legislation being mainly in the line of police regulations to prevent their running away.

New Hampshire from the first tended to discourage

[3] A. B. Hart, *Commonwealth History of Massachusetts* (New York: The States History Company, 1927), I, 269.
[4] *Suppression of the African Slave Trade*, p. 34.

slavery, but in course of time the system was recognized. An act passed in 1714 regulated the conduct of slaves, and one four years later the conduct of masters.

(c) The Middle Colonies. Slavery began in New York under the Dutch rule and continued under the English. Before, or about, 1650 the Dutch West India Company brought slaves to New Netherland. Most of these continued to belong to the Company, though after a period of labor some of the more trusty were allowed to have small farms, from the produce of which they made return to the Company. Their children were still slaves. In 1664 New Netherland became New York, and by an enactment the next year bond slavery was recognized.

In Maryland an act of 1663-1664 declared that all Negroes or other slaves imported into the province should serve for the term of their lives, and that their children should also serve for life.

Records of the beginnings of slavery in Delaware and in New Jersey are somewhat hazy, but in general it appears that the lot of those in bondage was somewhat better than elsewhere. Delaware was influenced to some extent in her views by Pennsylvania, and that colony was outstanding in the early years for its opposition to the enslavement of Negroes.

Protest against the slave system was first recorded in Pennsylvania, in 1688, when a memorial against it was drawn up by Francis Daniel Pastorius for the Germantown Quakers. In 1700 the legislature forbade the selling of slaves out of the province without their consent, and in 1705 prohibited their importation from Carolina.

(d) The South. In North Carolina, where there were many small farms and where there was not so much emphasis on large plantations as in colonies farther south, the system of human bondage was long controlled by custom rather than by legal enactment. It was recognized by law in 1715, however, and police laws to govern the life of slaves were enacted.

In South Carolina the natural resources made Negro slavery on a large scale profitable and explicit laws were formulated early. Slaves were first imported from Barbados, and their status received official confirmation in 1682. By 1720 the number had increased to 12,000, the white people numbering only 9,000. As early as 1698 fear of the preponderance of the Negro population was such that a special act was passed to encourage white immigration. Legislation "for the better ordering of slaves" was passed in 1690, and in 1712 the first regular slave law was enacted. Prohibitive duties from time to time guarded against too rapid increase, but by 1734 importation had again reached large proportions; and in 1740, in consequence of several insurrections, especially one led by a slave named Cato, a prohibitive duty much larger than any previous one was placed upon Negroes brought into the province. In general, in South Carolina slavery was very profitable not only because the natural resources were adapted to the plantation system which could employ unskilled slave labor on a large scale, but because the Negroes were naturally adapted to life in the hot, moist lowlands.

In Georgia, which was chartered in 1732 and founded the next year to carry out James Oglethorpe's plan to provide a refuge for persecuted Protestants and the debtor classes of England, slavery was slow to gain a foothold. It was forbidden on the ground that Georgia was to defend the other English colonies from the Spaniards on the south, and that the colonists would not be able to do this if, as in South Carolina, they dissipated their energies in guarding Negro slaves. For years the development of the province was slow, and the prosperous condition of South Carolina constantly suggested to the planters that "the one thing needful" for their highest welfare was slavery. Again and again petitions were addressed to the trustees; moreover, Negroes were sometimes hired for life, and purchases were openly made in Savannah. In 1749 the trustees formally yielded to the request, and in 1765 a slave code was adopted in what was destined to become one of the most important of the Southern states.

(e) Florida and Louisiana. In two colonies not in the original thirteen, but important in the later history of the United States, Negroes were present at a very early date, in the Spanish colony of Florida from the first and in the French colony of Louisiana as soon as New Orleans really began to grow. In 1721 there were 600 Negroes in Louisiana; by 1745 the number had increased to 2,020. The stories connected with these people are as tragic and as romantic as any in the history of the colony. In 1730 there was an insurrection led by a strong and desperate slave named Samba. This failed, but one of the most interesting things about it was that it gave suggestion of the possible alliance in the future of the Negro and the Indian.

7. Servitude and Slavery.   Negro slavery was not the only sort of bondage known in America in the seventeenth and eighteenth centuries. It was, in fact, partly because of a system already in existence that slavery became permanently fixed in the colonies. This system was known as *servitude* or *indenture,* and it explains many of the early acts with reference to the Negroes, especially those about intermarriage with white people. Servitude was "a legalized status of Indian, white, and Negro servants preceding slavery in most, if not all, of the English mainland colonies." [5]

For the origins of the system one must go back to social conditions in England in the seventeenth century. Throughout that century the lot of the workingman, especially of the agricultural laborer, left much to be desired. In the earlier years mowers received for a day's work what would be now from 8 to 25 cents. Rents constantly increased, and many persons died simply from starvation. In the hard times pressing upon them many Englishmen, hearing of the great undeveloped country of Virginia, determined to try their lot across the sea. Hundreds, however, were too poor to pay for their transportation, and accordingly sold themselves into servitude for a number of years to pay for the transfer. Perhaps even more important from the standpoint of servitude itself was the number of persons brought to America by involuntary means. Political offenders, vagrants, and criminals were thus sent to the colonies, and many persons, especially boys and girls, were kidnaped

[5] From the article, "Slavery," *New International Encyclopedia,* XXI, 166.

in the streets of London and "spirited" away. Indentured servants were purchased by the planters in the colonies either from kidnapers or from the government, the term of servitude being generally five or seven years.

In the laws made for the regulation of the conduct of indentured servants may be found the germ of all the slave codes of the colonies. As having the status of an apprentice, the servant could sue in court and was even allowed "freedom dues" at the expiration of his term. He could not, however, bear weapons and, of course, could not vote or hold office. The first Negroes who came to the country were technically servants. As slavery advanced white servitude declined; and servitude became slavery when "statutory law and court decisions added to such incidents of servitude as alienation, whipping, disfranchisement, limited marriage, trade, etc., first the incident of perpetual service and then a denial of civil and juridical capacity, as well as of marriage, property, and the possession of children." [6] The decline of the indenture system after the seventeenth century was very rapid, though it did not pass in all its phases before the beginning of the Revolutionary War.

8. Early Effort Toward Restriction. In spite of its economic advantage over white servitude, the system of Negro slavery did not develop without considerable opposition. Germantown's protest, made in the year 1688, was "the first formal action ever taken against the barter in human flesh within the boundaries of the United

[6] From the article, "Slavery," *New International Encyclopedia,* XXI, 166.

States." [7] In places other than Pennsylvania there developed sentiment against the institution; but even when an individual colony was impelled by philanthropic motives, it had to reckon with the cupidity of English traders. Before 1772 Virginia passed thirty-three acts looking toward a prohibition of the importation of slaves, but in every instance the act was disallowed by England. In the far South, especially in South Carolina, where the Negroes outnumbered the white people, constant fear of insurrections led to increasingly heavy duties on slaves imported. Yet in spite of all such spasmodic attempts at restriction, the system of Negro slavery, once well started, developed apace.

9. The Status of the Slave. The rise of the slavery system was distinctively an evolution. As the first Negroes were taken by pirates, the rights of ownership could not legally be given to those who purchased them; hence slavery by custom preceded slavery by statute. Little by little the colonies drifted into legalization of the sterner system, the transition being marked by such acts as that in Rhode Island, which permitted a Negro to be bound for ten years.

By the time that it had become generally enacted or understood in the colonies that a child born of slave parents should serve for life, a new question had arisen, that of the issue of a free person and a slave. This led Virginia to pass an act in 1662 to the effect that the status of a child should be determined by that of the mother, which act both gave to slavery the sanction

[7] A. B. Faust, *The German Element in the United States* (Boston: Houghton Mifflin Company, 1909), I, 45.

of law and made it hereditary. In 1705 it was further
enacted in Virginia that a slave might be inventoried
as real estate. As a man in bondage was then legally
regarded as property, there was nothing to prevent him
from being separated from his family. The colonists
found, however, that they were not dealing simply with
property, but with human beings; and in Virginia, which
in so many ways had taken the lead, some attempt seems
to have been made in 1801 to prevent the separation of a
young child from its mother.

In Maryland the problem of the relation of the Negro
slave and the indentured white servant was unusually
acute. A section of the law of 1664, designed to discourage the intermarriage of white women and Negro slaves,
enacted that a white woman so marrying should serve
the master of her husband as long as her husband lived,
and that the issue of such marriages should be slaves for
life. An interesting situation then developed. In order
to prolong the indenture of their white female servants,
many masters encouraged them to marry Negro slaves.
To prevent this, a new act in 1692 declared that all
white women so intermarrying should be free at once,
but that the master or mistress promoting the marriage
and the minister performing the ceremony were each
to pay a fine of ten thousand pounds of tobacco.[8] In
general in the Southern colonies the rule in the matter
of the child of the Negro father and the indentured
white mother was that the child should be bound in

[8] "An Act Concerning Negro Slaves," *Archives of Maryland*
(Baltimore: Maryland Historical Society, 1894), XIII (1684-1692),
549.

servitude for thirty or thirty-one years. With the passing of the system of servitude passed also for the most part the intermarriage of the races.

As a slave the Negro had none of the ordinary civil and personal rights of a citizen. In a criminal case he could be arrested, tried, and condemned with but one witness against him, and he could be sentenced without a jury. In the matter of religion and baptism a peculiar problem arose. Zealous for religion as the colonists were, they made little attempt to convert the Negroes in the earlier decades of the seventeenth century, there being a general opinion that neither Christian brotherhood nor the law of England would justify the holding of Christians as slaves. In the course of time they lost their scruples, and it became understood that conversion and baptism did not make a slave free, Virginia in 1667 passing a law to this effect.

Generally it was only on the economic side that any hope at all remained for the slave. Sometimes he was allowed to hire out his time. If he earned more than the sum (about $100) yearly due his master, he might begin to accumulate a little money on his own account and perhaps ultimately purchase his freedom. Such cases, however, were exceptional. For the great mass of Negroes in the colonies the outlook seemed almost completely hopeless.

10. The First Blows for Liberty. The Negroes who came to America from Africa in the eighteenth century were strikingly different from those whom generations of bondage later made comparatively docile. They were turbulent in disposition and likely at any moment to take

of it. Generally in the South Negroes could not vote, could not give testimony in court in cases involving white men, and could be employed only for fatigue duty in the militia. They could not purchase white servants, could not intermarry with white people, and had also to be very circumspect in their personal relations with slaves. No deprivation of privilege, however, relieved them of the obligation to pay taxes. Such advantages as the free Negro possessed were mainly economic. The money gained from his labor was his own; he might become skilled at a trade and find good employment; he might buy land; he might buy his wife and child if, as most frequently happened, they were slaves; in some sections he might even purchase slaves; and he might have one gun with which to protect his home.[14] Once in a long while he might find some private opportunity for education. In the North his political condition was somewhat better than in the South, and more avenues of education were open to him, but along economic lines his lot was harder.

Everywhere the free Negro's position was a difficult one. He was often regarded as idle and shiftless, and as a breeder of mischief; but if he showed unusual thrift he might be forced to leave his home and go elsewhere. Liberty, the boon of every citizen, the free Negro did not possess. For all the finer things of life—the things that make life worth living—the lot that was his was only less hard than that of the slave.

[14] Hening, *Statutes at Large*, IV, 131.

CHAPTER II

THE ERA OF THE REVOLUTION

13. The Character of the Age. The period of the American Revolution in its widest limits may include that of the War of 1812 as well as that of the Revolution itself. The progress of the cause of the Negro in this period is to be explained by two great forces which were being felt at the time in Europe as well as in America. One of these was the humanitarian impulse, which found expression in the poems of William Cowper. The other was the general diffusion of liberal ideas, which in England caused the agitation for a free press and for parliamentary reform, which in France accounted largely for the French Revolution, and which in America led to the break with Great Britain. No patriot could come under the influence of either of these forces without having his heart and his sense of justice moved to some degree in behalf of the slave.

14. Lord Mansfield's Decision. In November, 1769, Charles Stewart, once a merchant in Norfolk and later receiver general of the customs of North America, took to England his African slave, James Somerset, who, becoming sick, was turned adrift by his master. Later, when Somerset recovered, Stewart seized him, intending to have him borne out of the country and sold in Jamaica. The Negro, with strong assistance from English liberals, objected, and by so doing raised the legal question, Did a slave by being brought to England become free? This question had come up before but had not been formally passed upon. The Somerset case attracted the greatest attention, for everyone realized that the decision would be far-reaching. After the case had been argued at three different sittings, Lord Mansfield, Chief Justice, in 1772 handed down from the Court of King's Bench a decision that said in part: "The state of slavery is of such nature, that it is incapable of being introduced on any reasons, moral or political, but only by positive law . . . It is so odious that nothing can be suffered to support it, but positive law. Whatever inconveniences, therefore, may follow from the decision, I cannot say this case is allowed or approved by the law of England; and therefore the black must be discharged." [1] As commonly stated this meant that as soon as a slave set foot on the soil of England he became free.

Cowper, in *The Task*, celebrated the decision in lines that became famous:

No: dear as freedom is, and in my heart's
Just estimation prized above all price,
I had much rather be myself the slave
And wear the bonds, than fasten them on him.
We have no slaves at home: then why abroad?
And they themselves once ferried o'er the wave
That parts us, are emancipate and loosed.
Slaves can not breathe in England; if their lungs
Receive our air, that moment they are free;
They touch our country, and their shackles fall.

[1] T. B. Howell, *A Complete Collection of State Trials* (London, 1816), XX (1772-1777), 82.

15. English Sentiment.   This decision may be taken as representative of the progress that the cause of the Negro was making in England at the time. Early in the eighteenth century sentiment against the slave trade began to develop among the Christian people of the country. Pamphlets telling of the evils of slavery were circulated, and as early as 1776 a motion for the abolition of the slave trade was made in the House of Commons. John Wesley preached against the system, Samuel Johnson was not less positive, and Adam Smith in *The Wealth of Nations* showed its ultimate expensiveness. The list of those who worked against the evil is a long one; but special mention must be made of two of the greatest friends of the slave—Thomas Clarkson and William Wilberforce. Clarkson was strong in investigation and in organizing the movement against slavery, and Wilberforce was the parliamentary champion of the cause. For twenty years, assisted by such debaters as Burke, Fox, and the younger Pitt, Wilberforce worked until on March 25, 1807, the bill for the abolition of the slave trade received the royal assent. Even then his work was not finished, as slavery itself was yet to be abolished in the English dominions. How that was done we shall see in a later chapter.

16. American Sentiment.   The high thought of England necessarily found reflection in America, where the logic of the position of the patriots forced them to defend the cause of liberty at all times. As early as 1774, largely through the influence of the Quakers, the first anti-slavery society was organized in Philadelphia, with Benjamin Franklin as its president. John Adams thought

that "every measure of prudence ought to be assumed
for the eventual total extirpation of slavery from the
United States." Thomas Jefferson denounced the system as endangering the principle of liberty on which
the state was founded, "a perpetual exercising of the
most boisterous passions, the most unremitting despotism
on the one part, and degrading submission on the other."
Patrick Henry declared, "I will not—I can not justify it!
I believe a time will come when an opportunity will be
offered to abolish this lamentable evil." Washington
desired nothing more than "to see some plan adopted
by which slavery may be abolished by law," and ultimately liberated his own slaves.

These noble sentiments made some progress, but in
general the people did not respond to the high thought
of the patriots. They were as yet moved by feelings of
interest rather than of humanity; and in 1785, in a letter
to La Fayette, Washington said that petitions for the
abolition of slavery presented to the Virginia legislature
could hardly obtain a hearing.

17. The Boston Massacre. Crispus Attucks. Trouble between the American colonies and England began soon
after 1761, when revenue officers were granted writs of
assistance, that is, warrants giving customs collectors
power to enter houses or shops to hunt for smuggled
goods. In 1765 came the Stamp Act, which was designed
to make the colonies pay for the support of the British
Army in America. From this time forth there was rest-
lessness, and in Boston, throughout the month of February, 1770, there were minor clashes between the
citizens and the soldiers.

Early in the night of March 5, as the result of an encounter between some young men and a sentry on duty in Dock Square, seven British soldiers, led by Captain Thomas Preston, came up King Street (now State) with fixed bayonets, clearing everything before them. Near the head of the street and in the heart of the city they were met by forty or fifty persons armed with clubs and other means of attack. The leader of the group was Crispus Attucks, a man of Negro descent, a giant in stature, who had seen service on a whaling ship. There was an order to fire. The first shot killed Attucks. The second slew Samuel Gray, who was stepping toward the falling leader. James Caldwell, a sailor, and Samuel Maverick, a youth of seventeen, were mortally wounded; and some other persons were injured, though not so seriously.

The people of Boston were aroused as never before; and "From that moment," said Daniel Webster in later years, "we may date the severance of the British Empire." In 1888 a monument to Attucks and his companions was erected on Boston Common, where it now stands facing Tremont Street.

18. The Negro in the War. In November, 1775, Lord Dunmore, the unpopular governor of Virginia, proclaimed freedom to all slaves who would fight against the American revolutionists. As a result of this action, numbers of Negroes joined the British ranks.

The colonies, filled with alarm, changed their attitude toward the slaves and began to permit Negroes to enlist, their masters receiving payment from the public treasury. Massachusetts, Connecticut, Rhode Island, New York,

Pennsylvania, Maryland, Virginia, and North Carolina thus accepted the services of slaves, and severe penalties were threatened upon those who took up arms against the American cause. It was designed to organize in the South an army of Negroes, and Colonel John Laurens of the Continental forces had charge of the project. Able-bodied slaves were to be paid for by Congress at the rate of $1,000 each, and one who served well to the end of the war was to receive his freedom and $50. South Carolina and Georgia, distrustful of the plan, did not encourage or co-operate with Laurens; so he did not succeed in his assignment. A total of about three thousand Negroes served in the American army.

Two individual acts of heroism in the war were especially noteworthy. At the Battle of Bunker Hill, when Major John Pitcairn of the British army was exulting in his expected triumph, Peter Salem, a Negro, rushed forward, shot him in the breast, and killed him. When Colonel William Barton of the American army undertook to capture General Richard Prescott while the royal forces were stationed at Newport, Rhode Island, his chief assistant—the man who actually captured Prescott in bed—was a Negro named Prince.

At the close of the conflict New York, Rhode Island, and Virginia freed their slave soldiers; but for the most part the system remained as before.

19. The First Steps toward Abolition. Naturally in the Revolutionary era there was considerable effort to regulate or to totally prohibit the slave trade. The first draft of the Declaration of Independence arraigned Great Britain as the real promoter of slavery in America.

Delaware's article against the slave trade was the first such article to appear in a state constitution; but, as we shall see later, it is to Vermont, still a territory at this time, that the honor of taking the first step for the abolition of slavery really belongs. In 1782 the old Virginia statute forbidding emancipation except for meritorious service was repealed. Within the next ten years, until it was again in force, private emancipations were frequent. Maryland passed acts similar to those in Virginia prohibiting the further introduction of slaves and removing restraints on emancipation. New York and New Jersey followed the example of Virginia and Maryland in prohibiting the further introduction of slaves, but general emancipation in these states was not declared for many years. In 1780, in spite of opposition because of the course of the war, the Pennsylvania Assembly passed an act forbidding the further introduction of slaves, and giving freedom to all persons thereafter born in the state. Similar provisions were enacted in Connecticut and Rhode Island in 1784. In Massachusetts as early as 1701 the town of Boston had instructed its representatives in the general assembly to propose "putting an end to Negroes being slaves"; but it was not until 1783 that it was finally decided that the declaration in the Massachusetts Bill of Rights to the effect that "all men are born free and equal" forbade slavery. In this year also New Hampshire incorporated in her constitution an article definitely prohibiting the system.

Far different was the course in the Southern states; and while the last Continental Congress, in legislating for the great Northwest Territory, declared that in that region there should be no slavery or involuntary servitude, it was also provided that fugitives from labor or service should be returned to their owners. Thus was paved the way for the first fugitive slave law.

However, some progress at least had been made. By the time the convention for the framing of the Constitution of the United States met in Philadelphia in 1787, at least two of the original thirteen states (Massachusetts and New Hampshire) had positively prohibited slavery, and in three others (Pennsylvania, Connecticut, and Rhode Island) gradual abolition was in progress.

20. The Constitution and Slavery.   Slavery was the cause of two of the three great compromises that entered into the making of the Constitution of the United States (the third, which was the first made, being the concession to the smaller states of equal representation in the Senate). South Carolina, with able representatives, largely dominated the thought of the convention, threatening not to accept the Constitution if there was not compliance with her demands. An important question was that of the representation of Negroes, the Southern states advocating representation according to numbers, slave and free, while the Northern states were in favor of the representation of free persons only. It was finally agreed to reckon three fifths of the slaves in estimating taxes and to make taxation the basis of representation. With reference to the slave trade a bargain was made between the commercial interests of the North and the slaveholding interests of the South, the granting to Congress of unrestricted power to enact navigation laws

being conceded in exchange for twenty years' continuance of the African slave trade.

The main agreements on the subject of slavery were thus finally expressed in the Constitution:

Representatives and direct taxes shall be apportioned among the several States which may be included within this Union, according to their respective numbers, which shall be determined by adding to the whole number of free persons, including those bound to servitude for a term of years, and excluding Indians not taxed, three-fifths of all other persons. (Art. I, Sec. 2.)

The migration or importation of such persons as any of the states now existing shall think proper to admit, shall not be prohibited by the congress prior to the year 1808, but a tax or duty may be imposed on such importation, not exceeding ten dollars on each person. (Art. I, Sec. 9.)

No person held to service or labor in one State, under the laws thereof, escaping into another, shall, in consequence of any law or regulation therein, be discharged from such service or labor, but shall be delivered up on claim of the party to whom such service or labor may be due. (Art. IV, Sec. 2.)

It will be observed that the word *slaves* occurs in no one of these articles. The framers of the Constitution did not wish to have their document formally recognize property in human beings.

21. Inventions.   Of incalculable significance in the history of the Negro in America was the series of inventions of the years 1767-1793. In 1768 Richard Arkwright, after a year of experimenting, set up in Preston in England his first spinning frame, which consisted mainly of two pairs of revolving rollers. About 1764

James Hargreaves, of England, invented the spinning jenny. In 1779 the principles of these two inventions were utilized by Samuel Crompton in his spinning mule, which had as its distinctive feature a spindle carriage which, receding so as to ease the strain of winding on the spindles, produced yarn suitable for the manufacture of fine muslins. In this same period the revolutionary discovery of the power of steam by James Watt, of Glasgow, was applied to cotton manufacture, and improvements were made in printing and bleaching. There yet remained one invention to become of signal importance to the South. Eli Whitney, a graduate of Yale, went to Georgia and was employed by the widow of General Nathanael Greene on her plantation. Realizing the need of some machine for the more rapid separating of cotton seed from the fiber, he labored until in 1793 he succeeded in making his cotton gin of practical value, though the tradition is persistent that the real credit for the invention belongs to a Negro on the plantation. The cotton gin created excitement throughout the South, soon being in use everywhere, and the cultivation and exporting of the staple grew by leaps and bounds. Thus at the very time that Northern states were abolishing slavery, an industry that had slumbered became supreme, and the fate of hundreds of thousands of slaves was sealed.

22. The Influence of Toussaint L'Ouverture. About this time there came into the notice of the world a man whose influence on the history of the United States has yet to be fully estimated.

The most important colonial possession of France was

Santo Domingo, which then included also the present Haiti. Slaves had been brought into the colony in such numbers that in 1791 there were on the island sixteen Negroes to one white man. The French slave code was not harsh, but its provisions were generally disregarded by the planters on the island. The result of this and of a vacillating attitude on the part of the Assembly in Paris was that in 1794 Toussaint L'Ouverture, the leader of Negro insurgents, became supreme on the island. British soldiers invited by the planters were forced to leave in 1798. Toussaint brought the island to a high degree of prosperity, showing great ability as a statesman; but in 1802 he was treacherously seized on a vessel by the emissaries of Napoleon, taken to France, and confined in a dungeon. This ended the career of the man who caused France to lose a colonial possession that at the time was most important, and obtained for the Negro race its first independent settlement outside of the continent of Africa.

In America the influence of the Negro chieftain's success in Santo Domingo strengthened the antislavery movement, became one of the reasons for the cheap selling of Louisiana, and rendered more certain the prohibition of the slave trade by the United States in 1807. A wave of fear swept over the South, and the voice of morality began to speak more loudly to the New England conscience. The effect on legislation was immediate; South Carolina, North Carolina, and Georgia passing more repressive measures, directed especially against the importation of West Indian Negroes.

23. New States and Territories.   In Washington's administration considerable discussion grew out of memorials presented to Congress for the suppression of the slave trade. These generally emanated from the Quakers in Pennsylvania, who were untiring in their efforts for freedom. Some influence came also from such an independent character as the itinerant preacher, Lorenzo Dow, originally of Connecticut, who prophesied dire calamities unless the country hastened to rid itself of the evil of human bondage.

Vermont, the first state after the original thirteen, was admitted to the Union in 1791. Her constitution, originally adopted in 1777, declared very positively against slavery, so that to this state really belongs the honor of being the first to prohibit and abolish the system. In 1799, after much debating, New York at last declared for gradual abolition. By the provisions those who were slaves were to continue such for life. Children born after the next July fourth were to be free but were to remain as apprentices with the owner of the mother, the men until they were twenty-eight years old and the women until they were twenty-five. New Jersey also declared for gradual abolition in 1804, and in 1803 Ohio was admitted as a free state.

Meanwhile there was reaction elsewhere. A fugitive slave law was passed in 1793; Kentucky in 1792 and Tennessee in 1796 were admitted as slave states; and when Georgia ceded to the United States the territory now comprising Alabama and Mississippi, she exacted from the Federal government an article favorable to slavery. While, moreover, in line with the stipulation in the Constitution, it was enacted that the importation of slaves should cease after December 31, 1807, smuggling continued, sometimes on a large scale. Louisiana was admitted as a slave state in 1812; Indiana as a free state in 1816; then Mississippi (slave) in 1817, Illinois (free) in 1818, and Alabama (slave) in 1819.

It will be observed that up to this time the balance had been fairly well preserved between the slave and the free states. The South, however, soon realized that it could not long maintain this balance because of the lack of territory and also by reason of the fact that the business of the North tended more than that of the South to make for rapid growth of population. Then came the application of Missouri for entrance; but with that event the history of slavery started on a new era, one destined not to be closed until the Negro was free.

24. The Decline of Great Convictions. We have seen that at the beginning of this period liberal ideas were dominant in both England and America. One of the sad features of the close of the era is the fading of the ideals that had inspired the patriots of the Revolution.

The energies of the young nation were being directed to the material development of the country. In the North there was a lull in the agitation, the meetings of anti-slavery organizations becoming intermittent. In the South the men of patriotism and responsibility found themselves in the grasp of a mighty evil which it was almost as difficult to shake off as to endure. In general the demands of interest were taking precedence over those of humanity, and increasing sensitiveness on the subject of slavery was felt.

Yet considerable advance had been made. Four states (Massachusetts, New Hampshire, Vermont, and Ohio) had definitely prohibited slavery, and generally throughout the North abolition was in progress.

CHAPTER III

BEGINNINGS OF SOCIAL IMPROVEMENT AND ORGANIZATION

25. The Beginning of Race Consciousness. Every great war in which the United States has engaged has resulted in political and social advance for the Negro. The reason for this is that, when a war is in progress, the life of a country is unsettled and the tempo accelerated, so that changes that otherwise might have taken decades come to pass within a year or two, or even within a few months. So it was with the American Negro in the era of the Revolution. For the first time in their history men who had been held in one place moved about, sometimes in considerable numbers, and they were free to exchange ideas with men from other places. Formed in units for the purpose of the war, they became accustomed to being and acting together. The new feeling gave impetus to co-operation along religious lines; it definitely accounted for the founding of the first lodge of Negro Masons in the country; and it was given assistance by the individual achievement of such figures as Phillis Wheatley and Benjamin Banneker. Thus, as the eighteenth century drew to a close, we may note a genuine beginning in racial consciousness.

26. Social Improvement. Meanwhile there was the beginning of an organized effort to improve the social condition of the Negro.

On January 1, 1794, delegates from nine societies organized in Philadelphia the American Convention of Abolition Societies. Some of the state organizations were very active, and they were especially interested in cases that came before the courts. In 1797 the New York Society reported 90 complaints of injustice, 36 persons freed, 21 cases still in suit, and others under consideration. The Pennsylvania Society reported that it had been instrumental in the liberation of "many hundreds" of persons. The different branches, however, were not satisfied with mere liberation; they did anything they could for the promotion of the welfare of the Negroes in their respective communities, each being expected to report to the Convention on the number of freedmen in its state and on their employment and conduct. From time to time also the general organization issued addresses to the people who were the special objects of its solicitude. A typical one of these exhorted them to attend to the duty of public worship, to teach their children useful trades, to be simple in dress and furniture, to refrain from the use of spirituous liquors, to observe the sacredness of family ties, and in general to be diligent in their callings and faithful in all the relations that they bore to society.

As early as 1704 a school for Negroes had been opened in New York by Elias Neau, a Frenchman who, after some years of imprisonment because of his Protestant faith, had come to the city to try his fortune as a trader.

Before the Revolution a similar school was founded in Philadelphia by Anthony Benezet, another French Protestant, who identified himself with the Quakers and whose will at his death in 1784 made further provision for education. There were also beginnings in other places. All told, by 1800 the Negro had received much more education than is commonly supposed.

27. Phillis Wheatley.   Within recent years considerable attention has been given to Jupiter Hammon, a dutiful Negro of Long Island, highly esteemed by his owners, who as early as 1761 printed as a broadside in New York a poem with the title, "An Evening Thought. Salvation by Christ with Penetential Cries." This was the first composition by a Negro printed within the present limits of the United States. For a long time, however, the career of Hammon as America's first Negro poet was completely eclipsed by that of Phillis Wheatley.

This talented young woman was born in Senegal, on the west coast of Africa, in or about 1753. Brought to Boston on a slave ship in 1761, she became the special servant of Mrs. Susannah Wheatley, wife of John Wheatley, a tailor. With the assistance of Mary Wheatley, a daughter in the family, Phillis learned to read, and within a few years she was composing verses after the manner of Pope. In 1773, after formal manumission, she went to England in the care of Nathaniel Wheatley, son of the family, a physician having advised that the air of the sea would improve her health. While abroad she was under the patronage of the Countess of Huntingdon, to whom a poem on the death of George

Whitfield, former chaplain of this lady, had introduced her. By her wit and modesty she made many friends, and among the presents showered upon her was one given by Brook Watson, Lord Mayor of London, a superb folio copy of *Paradise Lost*, which is now in the library of Harvard College. While she was in England arrangements were made for the publication of her little book, *Poems on Various Subjects*. Other poems were written later, among them "Liberty and Peace."

Another collection was contemplated, but this never saw the light. The illness of Mrs. Wheatley caused Phillis to hasten her return to America. This best friend died after a few months, in 1774, her husband in 1778; and the daughter of the family, who had married and left the old home, also died in 1778. Nathaniel Wheatley was living abroad. In her loneliness Phillis listened to the voice of John Peters, a ne'er-do-well; she married him in April, 1778. Hard times now came upon her, and her health declined. At last she was compelled to accept work as a drudge in a cheap boardinghouse. Two of her three children died before her, and the third lay with its mother in death December 5, 1784.

The poems of Phillis Wheatley have frequently been reissued. In her day she was regarded as a prodigy, and her strange career and her historical significance have at times perhaps caused undue importance to be attached to her work; but there can be no denying that she had remarkable facility as a writer or that her achievement helped the cause of the Negro. Within four years (1834-1838), when the antislavery agitation was rising to its height, not less than three editions of *Poems on Various*

Subjects appeared, and in the early years of the nineteenth century single pieces were sometimes used in
school readers. It is worth noting that the signature of
the author, wherever it has been preserved, uses the
spelling *Phillis*.

28. Benjamin Banneker. Benjamin Banneker was the
first American Negro who in a large way challenged the
world by the independent power of his intellect.

He was born in Maryland, November 9, 1731. On the
maternal side his grandfather was an African named
Banaky, a prince in his own land, and his grandmother
was Molly Welsh, a young English woman who, having
been bound in servitude for seven years, in course of
time herself owned and then liberated and married
Banaky. Benjamin's father, Robert, was also an African,
a man of energy and thrift, who on becoming free pre-
ferred to use his wife's surname rather than that of the
man to whom he had belonged.

In his early years Benjamin Banneker received at a
school near his home the rudiments of an education.
Being of an inventive turn of mind, he later made a
clock that not only kept time but also struck the hours.
When he was twenty-seven years of age, his father died,
leaving to him full responsibility for a well-stocked farm.
Up to the time he was forty he did not have opportunity
for the full development of his powers. In 1772, however, steps were taken for the erection of the flour mills
of Ellicott City near his home; and the proprietors, who
happened to be Quakers, were friendly and bought many
provisions for their workmen from his farm. In 1787
George Ellicott, having observed the Negro farmer's

interest in mathematics, loaned him some books and some astronomical instruments. Banneker so thoroughly mastered the books that in course of time he was able to point out errors in them. A new world was opened before him; and whereas he had formerly been addicted to strong drink, he now overcame the habit completely. In 1789, when a commission was appointed to survey the Federal Territory, later the District of Columbia, at the suggestion of Andrew Ellicott he became a member of the group. In 1791 he began the issuing of a series of almanacs, the first being that for the year 1792; and thenceforth he was referred to both at home and abroad as proof of the intellectual capacity of the Negro. He died in October, 1806. At the height of his career he was described as "a large man of noble appearance, with venerable hair, wearing a coat of superfine drab broad-cloth," [1] and again as "of black complexion, medium stature, of uncommonly soft and gentlemanly manners and pleasing colloquial powers." [2]

29. Gustavus Vassa.   Gustavus Vassa (1745-1801?) was not, strictly speaking, an American Negro; but he spent some years in bondage in the colonies along the seacoast, and a book that he published was frequently reissued in this country.

Born in Benin, a country west of the main channel of the lower Niger, he was kidnaped when eleven years of age and placed on a ship to be taken to America. For

[1] Phillips, P. Lee, "The Negro, Benjamin Banneker, Astronomer and Mathematician," *Records of the Columbia Historical Society*, XX (April, 1916), 119.

[2] Norris, J. Saurin, *A Sketch of the Life of Benjamin Banneker* (Baltimore: John D. Toy, 1854), 7.

a while he served on a plantation in Virginia; then he was with a British naval officer, who helped him to get an education; and later he worked on plantations and on vessels going to the West Indies as the slave of a Philadelphia merchant. This last master was considerate, helped him to purchase his freedom, and otherwise acted as his friend and adviser. After some years of work as a ship's steward, Vassa was converted to Methodism and settled in England to engage in antislavery effort. In 1790 he presented to Parliament a petition for the suppression of the slave trade. Two years later he was for a while a guest in the home of Thomas Hardy, secretary of the London Corresponding Society, an organization that was sympathetic with the revolution in France.

The Interesting Narrative of the Life of Oloudah Equiano, or Gustavus Vassa was first issued in two volumes in London in 1789. The author had editorial assistance on the work, and it is not likely that he selected the laudatory title; but the heart of the book is his own. The narrative has a continuous flow and a pictorial quality that not only carry conviction but enthrall the reader. Vassa's larger significance is that he helped to bring the cause of the Negro in America into touch with the liberal forces in the England of his day.

30. Paul Cuffe.   Paul Cuffe (1759-1817) was a man of remarkable initiative and public spirit. He was born on one of the Elizabeth Islands near New Bedford, Massachusetts. His father, Cuffe Slocum, an African, had purchased his freedom, and his mother, who was Ruth Moses before her marriage, was of Indian descent. When he was still a youth he persuaded his brothers to

drop their father's slave name and to use his Christian name as their surname. Being interested in navigation, Cuffe became a sailor on a whaling vessel when only sixteen years of age, and when twenty he went into business for himself. After some unhappy experiences, these including the capture of his goods by pirates, he was able to purchase a good-sized schooner, and by 1806 he was the owner of one ship, two brigs, and several smaller vessels, besides considerable property in houses and lands. More and more he enlarged his sphere of action, going with his Negro crew not only to the South and to the West Indies, but also to England and Africa.

In the history of the Negro, Paul Cuffe is remembered primarily for three things. As early as 1780 he and his brother John raised the question about paying taxes in Massachusetts when Negroes were denied the privilege of voting; later they presented a petition to the legislature; and it was largely through their effort that the Negro was given the suffrage in the state in 1783. Second, when a school was needed near his home and some of his neighbors seemed unwilling to move in the matter, Cuffe at his own expense built a school for the children of the vicinity. Finally, when in 1815 he had an understanding with the African Institution of England that he would take to Sierra Leone six or eight capable men who would instruct the colonists in agriculture and the mechanical arts, and when he found that a number of other persons were eager to go, he sailed on December 10 with a total of nine families and thirty-eight persons, spending nearly $4,000 on those who exceeded his instructions, all in the hope that he might thereby improve their condition. He left at his death an estate of $20,000, a sum far greater then than now, and it was largely through his discretion and upright character that there was founded in New Bedford a tradition of justice for all.

31. Prince Hall and the Masons.   Prince Hall (1748?-1807) was the son of an English father and a mulatto woman of Barbados. In 1765, when only seventeen years of age, he worked his way from Bridgewater, the capital of the island, to Boston. In Massachusetts he was impressed by the lowly estate of the people, and he threw himself with his whole heart into anything pertaining to their welfare. Physically small and of refined features and bearing, he would hardly seem to have been adapted to the leadership of untutored people in a dark day; but he had great moral force and the power to win the allegiance of men. He entered the Methodist ministry, and thenceforth took a positive stand on all questions relating to freedom and justice. In 1775, after vain attempts to get recognition from the American Masonic bodies, Prince Hall and fourteen of his black brethren were initiated in a British army lodge attached to a regiment stationed near Boston. In March, 1784, these men applied to the Grand Lodge of England for a warrant. This was issued in the following September to "African Lodge, No. 459," with Prince Hall as master. Delays befell the warrant, but organization was at last effected on May 6, 1787. The founding of this lodge marked not only the beginning of Masonry among the Negro people of America, but also one of the earliest attempts at co-operative effort on the part of American Negro men outside the field of the church.

32. The Origins of the Negro Church. The Moravians, or United Brethren, were the first Christians who attempted the establishment of missions for Negroes, and the Presbyterians began work in 1735; but, not unnaturally, it was the democratic Baptist denomination that led in the founding of distinctively Negro churches. There has been much discussion as to which was the first Negro Baptist church, and claims have been put forward for organizations in Petersburg, Virginia, Williamsburg, Virginia, and Savannah, Georgia, founded in 1776 or very soon thereafter; but students of the subject have shown that there was a Negro Baptist church at Silver Bluff on the South Carolina side of the Savannah River, in Aiken County, just twelve miles from Augusta, Georgia, founded not earlier than 1773, not later than 1775.[3] St. Thomas's Episcopal Church in Philadelphia was organized in 1791, and Bethel Church in the same city in 1794.

The Methodists, while not quite as numerous as the Baptists, call for special consideration by reason of important branches in the denomination. The parent organization was that founded by John Wesley, the Methodist Episcopal Church. In 1787, in protest against the indignities they had to suffer, the Negroes who had been worshiping in St. George's Methodist Episcopal Church in Philadelphia, left the edifice during a service, led by

[3] Walter H. Brooks, *The Silver Bluff Church* (Washington, 1910), pp. 5, 16. See also M. M. Fisher, *A Short History of the Baptist Denomination* (Nashville: Sunday School Publishing Board, 1933), pp. 35, 39.

Richard Allen and Absalom Jones. They organized the Free African Society, and out of the movement came in 1791 St. Thomas's Episcopal Church, of which Jones became rector, and the African Methodist Episcopal Church which was organized in 1816 as a distinct denomination, Allen becoming the first bishop. It was Allen, a man of strict integrity and indomitable perseverance, who led in the founding of Bethel Church. In 1820 a union of churches in and near New York resulted in the formation of the African Methodist Episcopal Zion Church. The polity of this organization is slightly different from that of the A. M. E. Church. The laymen are represented in the conferences, and there is no bar to the ordination of women. The beginning of a third group of Negro Methodists takes us some years beyond this point in our story but might best be mentioned here. In 1844, because of the increasing difference between the North and the South on the subject of slavery, there was a division in the main body of the Methodist Episcopal Church, and the Methodist Episcopal Church, South, resulted. Considerable work for the Negroes was done by this latter organization before the Civil War, the distinctively racial churches not then being able to advance in the South. When the war was over, however, and the way was clear for them, the Methodist Episcopal Church, South, observed a great withdrawal of its Negro communicants to the A. M. E. and A. M. E. Z. churches. Accordingly it deemed it wise to establish in 1870 its own Negro branch; and thus came into existence the Colored Methodist Episcopal Church, commonly known as the C. M. E. Church. All along, of course, a great many Negroes remained in the parent body, the Methodist Episcopal Church. Accordingly, in later years, aside from smaller bodies, we had Negro Methodists in four denominations, three being distinctively racial—the African Methodist Episcopal Church, the African Methodist Episcopal Zion Church, the Colored Methodist Episcopal Church, and the Methodist Episcopal Church.

CHAPTER IV

THE INSTITUTION OF SLAVERY

33. A General View of the System. It is now time to inquire somewhat more intimately into the actual working of the system that was the dominant factor in the life of the Negro even until the Civil War.

There was marked difference between the type of bondage in the South and that in the North, though even in the North there was not always reasonable provision for the comfort of slaves in winter. In the far South the rapid importation into America of hosts of Africans, and the turbulent character of those who came, tended toward the development of harsh and even inhumane slave codes. On the other hand, in New England and New York the Negroes were for the most part house servants or farm hands, and they were treated very much like other servants in their day. "Between these two extremes, the system of slavery varied from a mild serfdom in Pennsylvania and New Jersey to an aristocratic caste system in Maryland and Virginia." [1]

For a long time it cost as much to raise a slave as he would ultimately be worth, and it was commonly thought to be cheaper to buy those who were to labor than to rear them. The legal abolition of the slave trade, however, and the heavy demands imposed by the Louisi-

[1] DuBois, *Suppression of the African Slave-Trade*, p. 6.

ana Purchase and the development of the lower South, greatly changed matters. The slave increased in value, and Virginia and Maryland became breeding places for the plantations in Georgia and Alabama. In the decade before the Civil War considerably more than twenty thousand slaves a year were exported to the cotton states: a contemporary authority gives "the annual importation of slaves, for the ten years ending 1860, into seven of the Southern Slave States from the Slave-breeding States as 26,301." [2] It was the rude severing of family ties thus entailed that made the system odious to many even in the South.

34. Procuring Slaves. The actual procuring of slaves was by no means as easy as is sometimes supposed. The captain of a vessel had to resort to various expedients in order to get his cargo. His commonest method was to bring with him a variety of gay cloth, cheap ornaments, and whisky, which he would give in exchange for slaves brought to him. His task was most simple when a chieftain of one tribe brought to him several hundred prisoners of war. Most often, however, the work was more toilsome, and kidnaping was a favorite method, individuals frequently being enticed on vessels. The work was always dangerous, for after the natives along the coast had seen some of their kindred taken away, they armed themselves, and often there were hand-to-hand encounters.

"At first the slave vessels only visited the Guinea Coast, and bargained with the Negroes of the villages

[2] Frederick Law Olmsted, *The Cotton Kingdom*, I, 58 (see footnote).

there for what quantity of wax, or gold, or Negroes they had to give. But this was a clumsy way of conducting business. The ships had to sail along a large tract of coast, picking up a few Negroes at one place, and a little ivory or gold at another;—and even under the most favorable circumstances it took a considerable time to procure a decent cargo. No coast is so pestilential as that of Africa, and hence the service was very repulsive and very dangerous. As an improvement on this method of trading, the plan was adopted very early of planting small settlements of Europeans at intervals along the slave coast, whose business it should be to negotiate with the Negroes, stimulate them to activity in the slave-hunting expeditions, purchase the slaves brought in, and warehouse them until the arrival of the ships. These settlements were called slave factories. Factories of this kind were planted all along the western coast from Cape Verde to the equator by English, French, Dutch, and Portuguese traders." [3]

35. The Middle Passage. Once on board, the slaves were put in chains two by two. When the ship was ready to start, the hold of the vessel, whose ceiling might be just four or five feet from the floor, would be crowded with moody and unhappy wretches who most commonly were made to crouch so that their knees touched their chins. There was but one entrance to the hold, and the gratings on the sides were small. The food, such as it was, was not well prepared, nor was any care taken to see that all were fed. The supply of water was always limited, a pint a day being a generous allowance. Sleep-

[3] Blake, *The History of Slavery and the Slave Trade,* p. 99.

ing conditions were horrible. Throughout the night the hold resounded with the moans of those who awoke from dreams of home to find themselves in bonds. The women frequently became hysterical, and both men and women sometimes became insane. Fearful and contagious diseases broke out. Smallpox was one of these. Very common was ophthalmia, a frightful inflammation of the eyes. Sanitary conditions can better be imagined than described. The putrid atmosphere, sudden transitions from heat to cold, and melancholy increased the mortality among a people naturally lighthearted; and frequently when morning came, a dead and a living slave would be found shackled together. The rule was to bring all in the hold to the deck for an airing twice a day, about eight o'clock in the morning and four in the afternoon; but, even so, a captain always counted on losing on the voyage one fourth of his cargo of slaves.

36. Prices of Slaves. Soon after a ship came to port, an auction would be announced. In the earlier years the price of a slave was far less than just before the Civil War; but consideration must be given to the greater purchasing power of money. About the year 1700 able-bodied adult Negroes were valued at from $150 to $200, and children at $50 or $60. There was little difference in the value of men and women, for, while a man might do more work, a woman might beget children for her master. A man worth $200 would in a very few seasons by his labor bring back to his owner the amount of money expended for him. After the invention of the cotton gin, the price of slaves rose rapidly; and by the middle of the nineteenth century, that for an able-bodied man or a beautiful woman was often $1,200, and, in exceptional cases, $1,800 or even more. A slave was regarded as personal property, and to steal one was a capital offense.

37. The Work of Slaves. Slaves were of most value when large numbers of them worked together. In the South, the tendency was to develop large plantations. One thousand was the number of slaves on the ordinary large plantation, though once in a while the figure became as high as four or even five thousand. The hands lived in the "quarters," a collection of rude, dilapidated cabins. In Virginia and Kentucky tobacco was raised. In South Carolina, the cultivation of rice began about 1693. For a long time indigo was next to this staple in importance, and some silk, flax, oranges, corn, and sugar were also raised; but, as we have seen, in the early years of the nineteenth century cotton became supreme.

The law with reference to slaves on plantations imposed a penalty of £5 if they were made to work on Sunday or more than fifteen hours a day in summer or fourteen in winter. This was for the colonial period, but the same general limits obtained in later years.

Such skilled labor as the South possessed before the Civil War was mainly in the hands of slaves, who might be blacksmiths, harness makers, brickmasons, or carpenters. Generally, however, work in the trades was such as was incident to plantation life. Almost nothing in the way of manufacturing was done in the South; and it was because goods were imported from England

and the North that Charleston was for so long a time a commercial city of commanding importance.

38. Laws Concerning Slaves. When it is remembered that each state had its own slave code, it will be seen that it is a difficult matter to make general statements about the legal side of slavery.

A man in bondage was by law due support in age or sickness, a right to limited religious instruction, and the privileges of marrying, having some free time, and testifying in cases concerning other slaves. If he did not get what was due him, he had no redress, for he had no legal voice. His marriage was not considered binding and he was not supposed to have any morals, though many individuals were models of integrity and faithfulness.

In New England, slaves were regarded as having the same legal rights as apprentices, and if masters abused their authority, they were liable to indictment.

The code of South Carolina may be taken as representative of the harsher ones. According to this a slave could not leave a plantation without a ticket of leave from his master; if he had no passport, he might be given twenty lashes, or be "moderately punished" by any man that stopped him, or be regarded as a fugitive.

He could have no firearms or other weapons in his possession; nor, for fear of poisonings, was he allowed to make any medicines without the knowledge of his master or mistress. On plantations no master was to allow a slave to plant for himself any corn, peas, or rice, or keep any private stock; and slaves were to wear clothes of the coarsest material only. Such provisions as these last, however, were frequently disregarded.

39. Punishment. By the South Carolina act of 1740, a fine of £700 was imposed for the deliberate murder of a slave by his master or another white man, £350 for killing him under correction or in the heat of passion, and £100 for mutilation or cruel punishment. In Mississippi, it was decided in 1820 that the wanton killing of a slave by his master was murder. In Georgia, however, it was declared thirty years later that a master had absolute power over a slave. In actual practice, as plantations were remote, no penalty was anywhere attached to the murder of a slave by his master, though of course the owner could sue for damages if the slave was killed by anybody else.

For stealing, the punishment of a slave most often was whipping. "The ordinary death penalty for the black man was hanging. Burning at the stake was not unknown, but there is one instance of such an execution in Massachusetts, and there are several in New York, so that it can not be cited as illustrating any peculiarity of the South Carolina type of slavery." [4]

40. Religion. Of the slaves who came to America a very few of the first were Mohammedans who could read the Koran. Most of them, however, were densely ignorant and very superstitious. They remained illiterate in this country as, except in some places in the North, it was a crime to teach a slave to read. On the matter of religion there seems from the first to have been some

[4] John Fiske, *Old Virginia and Her Neighbors* (Boston: Houghton Mifflin and Company, 1900), II, 311.

concern; indeed it was in the thought that in America the slave was brought into the light of Christianity that some people solaced themselves for the whole system of human bondage. In cities, slaves were expected to go to church, and there they occupied a corner or a gallery. On plantations it was common for the hands to have a meeting on Sunday, and it was at this that the "exhorter" fulfilled his wonted function. The law required that at least one white person should be present at any such meeting, but in actual practice an overseer simply looked in for a moment to see that nothing unusual was being done. Much of the worship was the cultivation of emotional frenzy, but here and there light shone in the darkness and the true gospel was preached. The Negro church was born nearly a hundred years before the Civil War.

41. Peculiar Social Aspects. In the study of slavery, as in that of any other institution, it is to be remembered that peculiar attendant circumstances were ever present to modify large deductions that might be made. One thing that has been touched upon more than once in these pages is the differing character of slavery in different states, even in those in the South. On the great plantations along the coast or in the cotton belt, slavery appeared in all its grossness and hideousness. In Virginia, however, there was originally a more patriarchal form of the system, and the mistress of the estate not infrequently became the nurse of the slaves on the plantation. In numberless instances also, the masters of plantations themselves became the fathers of slaves. In general their children fared just like other slaves, but not always.

Such instances as these but emphasized the evil effects of slavery on both the dominant and the subject race.

42. Economic Failure of Slavery.   We have seen that on its own confession the colony of Georgia did not begin to grow until it used slave labor, and that in course of time the very life of the South came to depend on the cotton industry. The ultimate economic effects of the system of slavery on this section, however, were disastrous: "it needed no extensive marshalling of statistics to prove that the welfare of the North was greater than that of the South. Two simple facts, everywhere admitted, were of so far-reaching moment that they amounted to irrefragable demonstration. The emigration from the slave States to the free States was much larger than the movement in the other direction; and the South repelled the industrious emigrants who came from Europe, while the North attracted them." [5] The rich men of the South moreover invested their capital in land and slaves, so that mercantile interests passed into the hands of Northerners and Englishmen; and in course of time the South became wholly dependent on places outside of herself for manufactured goods. This fact accounts for South Carolina's attitude toward the tariff of 1828 and her emphasis on the principle of nullification. At the time when on account of increased production cotton was falling in value from forty cents a pound to seven or eight cents, this same cotton was coming back from England as cloth or clothing under a very high tariff.

[5] James Ford Rhodes, *History of the United States* (New York: The Macmillan Company, 1928), I, 355.

It was the rich planter rather than the white man of slender means who profited by slavery, wealth being more and more concentrated in a few hands. Among those white people who did not own slaves, also, there grew up a contempt for industrial effort, all manual labor being associated in their minds with slavery. In 1860, 41 per cent of the white men who had been born in South Carolina were living in other states.[6] Some of the men of Scotch-Irish stock in the "up-country" emigrated before the middle of the century on account of antipathy to slavery, and still others were attracted to the rich lands of the West; but the great majority of those who moved were driven away by the competition of slave labor.

More and more the South realized that she was not keeping pace with the country's development. Virginia, that before the Revolution and up to the adoption of the Federal Constitution contained more wealth and a larger population than any other state, by 1852 had fallen to fifth place in wealth and fourth in political power.[7] The apologist for current conditions might have shown more than one reason for this decline, but students of political economy agreed upon one main cause, and that was slavery.

[6] As stated in a newspaper article by Professor D. D. Wallace, in the Columbia *State* (Columbia, South Carolina), August 15, 1909.
[7] Richmond *Enquirer* (Richmond, Virginia), December 25, 1852.

CHAPTER V

THE NEGRO'S REACTION TO SLAVERY

43. The Outlook for the Slave. To the Negro in bonds the institution of slavery was one long night with little hope of day. His highest impulses, his tenderest emotions, and every incentive to noble endeavor, felt the blasting effects of the system. He might work in the field from sunrise to sunset, but none of the fruit of his labor was his own. He might cherish the instincts of a father, only to see his child torn from his arms forever. He might possess lofty ambition or even genius, and find effort made to deprive him of every quality of manhood. With his brethren he sang his "sorrow song," "I've been a-listenin' all the night long"; and in yearning for the joys of heaven he prayed for deliverance from physical bondage. To escape at once, however, was possible only by regular manumission, by open revolt, or by running away.

It is the purpose of this chapter to review some of the efforts put forth by the Negroes themselves to cast off the chains that bound them and to have some opportunity in education and culture.

44. Fugitives, Indian and Negro. In spite of the harsh laws against fugitives and the certain trail of bloodhounds, a great many slaves chose to run away. The attempt was commonly to direct one's way to the North, where the fugitive slave law of 1793 was not generally in force. Traveling largely by night under the guidance of the North Star, the Negroes sustained themselves as best they could.

The Dismal Swamp in Virginia became a famous hiding place. A colony here defied owners right in the midst of a strong slavery community. Soldiers never ventured into the colony, and bloodhounds sent thither did not return.

As many of the slaves made their way to Canada, an attempt was made in 1828 to effect some arrangement with Great Britain for the return of those who escaped thither; but this failed.

In the far South, while Florida was still under Spanish rule, there was also some question, as many fugitives took refuge and intermarried with the Indians. In 1816 American troops blew up a fort on the Appalachicola that was the headquarters of many slaves who had run away; and the first Seminole War was very largely caused by fugitives. When Florida was annexed slave-hunting increased, and then the escaping Negroes made their way as far south as the Everglades. The second Seminole War was even more directly caused by fugitives than the first. The famous leader Osceola had a wife who was the daughter of a woman of Negro descent who had found refuge with the Indians. One day in 1835 while at Fort King, the wife was seized, being claimed as a slave by her mother's former owner. Osceola vowed revenge, and was temporarily imprisoned. On being released he conducted the war with remarkable bravery and resource, and it stands to the shame of American arms that he was captured under a flag of truce and died in imprisonment.

45. **Insurrections. Denmark Vesey.** We have already considered some of the very early attempts of slaves to free themselves by force. More ambitious in scope than any effort that had preceded it was the attempt made in Richmond, Virginia, in 1800 and known as Gabriel's Insurrection. This was planned by two young and intelligent men, Gabriel Prosser, who was twenty-four years old, and Jack Bowler, who was twenty-eight. These leaders organized as many as 1,000 Negroes in Henrico County, who were to march in three columns on the city and seize the arsenal. A slave named Pharaoh divulged the plot; moreover, a great storm on the day appointed washed away bridges and inundated the meeting place. Gabriel was captured in Norfolk after a little more than three weeks, and he and more than a score of his followers were executed. The effort was thus a failure; nevertheless, coming as it did so soon after the revolution in Haiti, and giving evidence of young and unselfish leadership, it was regarded as of extraordinary significance.

Even more carefully matured was the plan of Denmark Vesey in Charleston, South Carolina, in 1822. This man, originally from the West Indies, was gifted with remarkable sagacity and personal magnetism. In 1800, at the age of thirty-three, by winning a prize in a lottery he found himself in possession of $1,500. Of this amount he paid $600 for his liberty; then, working at his trade, carpentry, he won general esteem. In course of time he conceived a plan that contemplated nothing less than the annihilation of the white population of Charleston. Aided by five capable associates, Peter Poyas, Rolla Bennett, Ned Bennett, Monday Gell, and Gullah Jack, he brought into his plan thousands of Negroes in the city and outlying districts, upon whom all the while the greatest secrecy and strict attention to daily tasks were enjoined. Vesey at length selected a Sunday night in July as the time for his attack, Sunday because on that day many Negroes from the plantations would be in the city, and July because in midsummer many of the white people were away. Of one class of slaves he had a peculiar distrust. "Take care," he said, "and don't mention the plan to those waiting men who receive presents of old coats, etc., from their masters, or they'll betray us." That his suspicions were justified was proved late in May when one of those very "waiting men" endeavored to inform against him but was baffled. The plan was now hastened by four weeks, Sunday, June 16, being the new date. Again in a few days it was divulged by a "waiting man," one who had more accurate knowledge than the first informant. The attempt to carry out the plan was easily suppressed, and the chief figures were tried before a special court in which Robert Y. Hayne appeared against them. Vesey conducted his case with great skill but was finally condemned to death. With Spartan courage Peter Poyas said to his associates, "Do not open your lips! Die silent as you shall see me do." In all, thirty-five men were executed and forty-three banished. Thus closed the insurrection that, for the magnitude of its plan, the care with which it was matured, and the faithfulness of the leaders to one another, was never equaled by a similar revolt of the Negro against slavery in the United States.[1]

46. Nat Turner. The most famous of the Negroes who struck for freedom was Nat Turner, who was typical of the emotional insurrectionist just as Vesey was of the intellectual.

This man was born in Virginia, in Southampton County, and in his early years learned to read with such rapidity that he was regarded as a prodigy. From his childhood he believed that he was divinely chosen for some great mission, and he said that he heard voices and had visions, one dream being of white and black spirits contending in battle. Though he thus lived so largely in a mystical world, he was not formally a preacher. It is recorded of him that he was never known to swear an oath, to drink a drop of spirits, or to commit a theft. Instead he cultivated fasting and prayer and the reading of the Bible.

In course of time he became convinced that it was the will of God that he should free his people; and an eclipse in February, 1831, was accepted as the sign for which he had been waiting. This was reinforced by a peculiar appearance of the sun on August 13. On the night of Sunday, August 21, after long conference with

[1] The two original sources of information about Denmark Vesey's insurrection are related: *An Official Report of the Trials of Sundry Negroes* by Lionel H. Kennedy and Thomas Parker and *An Account of the Late Intended Insurrection among a Portion of the Black of this City*, both published at Charleston in 1822, the latter by authority of the Charleston Corporation. For more extended accounts of both this and the Nat Turner insurrection, with special bibliographies, see Brawley, *A Social History of the American Negro,* pp. 132-148, 405-407.

his chief associates—Henry Porter, Hark Travis, Nelson
Williams, Sam Francis, and Will Francis, the last a man
of gigantic frame—Turner began his work with the
killing of the five members of the family of his master,
Joseph Travis. Throughout the early hours of Monday
morning the bloody work continued, the insurrectionists
meanwhile increasing in number. Prominent among the
events of the morning was the killing at one home of
ten children who were gathering for school. In all,
fifty-seven white persons were killed, and more would
doubtless have lost their lives if their slaves had not
defended them. By noon the news had spread. United
States troops came from Fortress Monroe, and the
militia from different counties in Virginia and North
Carolina. After Turner had succeeded in concealing
himself for more than two months, he was finally discovered, tried, and hanged. As he predicted, the day of
his death was one of terrible thunder and lightning. Not
less than twenty of his associates were also hanged,
but this number takes no account of the scores of
Negroes illegally killed.

The insurrection created the wildest excitement
throughout the South. Near Fayetteville, North Carolina, the white women and children were so panic-
stricken that they took refuge in the swamps, from
which they returned after two days, muddy, chilled,
and half-starved. The effects on legislation were immediate; the slave codes were made more harsh and the
disabilities of free Negroes were increased.

47. **David Walker's** *Appeal.* In 1829, just two years
before Nat Turner's insurrection, there appeared in

Boston a remarkable publication, *Walker's Appeal, in Four Articles; together with a Preamble, to the Coloured Citizens of the World, but in Particular and very Expressly to Those of the United States of America.*

This book was the work of David Walker, a man who had been born in Wilmington, North Carolina, in 1785 of a free mother and a slave father, and who soon felt such detestation for the whole system of human bondage that he resolved not to live in the South. Making his way to Boston, he opened a clothing store and prospered, all the while showing interest in the poor and needy of his people. He was described as six feet in height, slender, well proportioned, and dark, with loose hair. His book severely arraigned the ignorance and cruelty engendered by slavery; it exposed the hypocrisy of many who professed to follow Jesus Christ, and very strongly it opposed the plan for colonization, of which we shall hear more in the next chapter.

The governors of Virginia and North Carolina sent special messages to their legislatures about the publication, and the governor of Georgia wrote to Harrison Gray Otis, mayor of Boston, to ask that it be suppressed. Otis replied that personally he did not approve of the pamphlet, but that the author had not done anything that made him amenable to law. A reward of a thousand dollars was then offered for Walker's head, the amount to be ten times as much if he was taken alive. His wife and friends advised him to go to Canada, but he refused, saying, "I will stand my ground. Somebody must die in this cause." Before the close of 1830 he was dead, and naturally the belief was that he met with foul play from the forces that had threatened his life.

Within little more than a year, however, his book was in the third edition, and it has the importance of being the boldest and most direct appeal for freedom of which we hear in the earlier years of the century.

48. The *Amistad* Incident. Important by reason of its legal consequences, was an occurrence that happened in 1839, on a Spanish slave schooner, *L'Amistad*, sailing from Havana for Guanaja in the vicinity of Puerto Principe. On the night of June 30, under the leadership of one of their number named Cinque, the fifty-three slaves on board rose against the crew, killed the captain, with a slave that belonged to him, and two sailors; and, while they permitted most of the crew to escape, they took into close custody the two men, Jose Ruiz and Pedro Montes, who were supposed to be their owners. Montes, who had some knowledge of nautical affairs, was ordered to steer the vessel back to Africa. So he would by day, when the Negroes were watching him, but at night he tried to make his way to some land nearer at hand. At length, on August 26, the schooner was captured off Long Island by the United States brig *Washington*, commanded by Captain Gedney, who secured the Negroes and took them to New London, Connecticut, to await trial. The Spanish minister, Calderon, demanded that they be surrendered as "property rescued from pirates," and the American Secretary of State, John Forsyth, was disposed to comply with the request. The suggestion, however, met with violent opposition from the antislavery element. For a year and a half the matter dragged through legal technicalities and differences, the friends of the Negroes meanwhile teaching them to read so that they could tell their story without an interpreter. Early in 1841 the case reached the United States Supreme Court, before which a former president, John Quincy Adams, appeared in behalf of the captives. His argument covers 135 octavo pages, and he showed among other things that the slave trade was illegal by international agreement, so that the only thing to do under the circumstances was to release the Negroes. After a decision was rendered in his favor, Lewis Tappan, one of the organizers of the New York Anti-Slavery Society, raised money for the transportation of the group back to Africa.

In November, 1841, a somewhat similar incident occurred while one hundred and thirty slaves were being taken from Virginia to New Orleans on the brig *Creole*. Madison Washington, one of their number, organized a rebellion and took possession of the vessel, carrying it to Nassau, on New Providence, one of the Bahama Islands. The English authorities refused to surrender the Negroes.

49. The Convention Movement. While such insurrections as we have considered were significant, the number of Negroes who resorted to force for the improvement of their condition was, after all, comparatively small. A far greater number used the appeal to reason, with organization, agitation, and protest.

In 1817 the greatest excitement was created by a report that, through the efforts of the recently organized American Colonization Society, all free Negroes were forcibly to be deported from the country. Within the next twelve years the Missouri Compromise, Vesey's attempted insurrection, and the rising hostility between the slave and the free states, all led to far-reaching discussion, so that by 1830 feeling was acute throughout the country.

Men in such centers as New York, Philadelphia, and Baltimore were increasingly convinced that they should plan and work together; and in September, 1830, there was a preliminary gathering in Philadelphia. Out of this came in June, 1831, a meeting that extended over five days and that was formally known as the First Annual Convention of the People of Color. The very first resolution passed was, "That a committee be appointed to institute an inquiry into the condition of the free people of color throughout the United States, and report their views upon the subject at a subsequent meeting." Thus began a movement that continued, though sometimes with lapses, until the Civil War.

One of the most important projects considered in the earlier years was that of an industrial college, perhaps to be established in New Haven. By 1854 the founding of the Republic of Liberia had led to some modification of the original attitude of Negro men on colonization, and the whole question was considered on its merits, with investigation embracing not only Africa, but also the West Indies and Central and South America.

Among the men who came into prominence in these years were James McCune Smith, who in 1837 returned from the University of Glasgow with the degree of

Doctor of Medicine; James W. C. Pennington, a Presbyterian minister of New York, who had received the degree of Doctor of Divinity at Heidelberg; Martin R. Delany, an eager, restless spirit, passionately devoted to his people; and Henry Highland Garnet, a Presbyterian minister who saw service in New York and Washington and closed his career as Minister to Liberia. Garnet was in spirit the successor of David Walker, whose *Appeal* he brought out in a new edition in 1848.

50. **Frederick Douglass.** Most famous of all the Negroes of the period was Frederick Douglass (1817-1895). This man was born at Tuckahoe, Talbot County, Maryland, the son of an unknown white man and Harriet Bailey, a slave. In his early years he was taken to Baltimore as a servant, but he learned his letters and became eager for an education. When about thirteen years of age he secured a copy of a book of speeches, *The Columbian Orator*, and the stirring appeals for liberty awoke in him something that he never lost.

In 1838, when working as a calker in Baltimore, where he was permitted to hire his time, he made his escape from slavery, going first to New York and thence to New Bedford. In the latter city he was befriended by a public-spirited Negro, Nathan Johnson, who, from a reading of Scott's *The Lady of the Lake*, suggested the name *Douglas*. This was adopted, though later the spelling was always with a double *s*. For three years the young man worked without a vacation about the docks of New Bedford; then, in the summer of 1841, when he was twenty-four years of age, having read the *Liberator* issued by Garrison, he thought he would take a few days off to attend an antislavery convention in Nantucket, Massachusetts. An abolitionist, William C. Coffin, who had heard him speak to the Negro people in New Bedford, sought him out in the crowd and asked him to say a few words. By his powerful physique and remarkable voice, he made an indelible impression; and, although he felt his need of education, he was persuaded to become, for at least three months, an agent of the Massachusetts Anti-Slavery Society.

Thenceforth he belonged to his people and the country. For four years he was under the tutelage of Garrison, and he lectured extensively in the North and East. In 1845 he went to England, where he remained two years, meeting prominent liberals, speaking to large audiences, and rapidly growing in intellectual stature. In order that there might be no question when he returned to America, English friends raised £150 to enable him to purchase his freedom. On his return to the United States Douglass began to issue in Rochester a weekly paper, *The North Star*, the name later being *Frederick Douglass' Paper*. The establishment of this periodical marked a break with Garrison, who stood aloof from politics. Thenceforth Douglass stood with those who sought the abolition of slavery by constitutional means. After the Civil War he conducted in Washington for three years another weekly, *The New National Era*, and later was United States marshal, recorder of deeds for the District of Columbia, and Minister to Haiti.

Perhaps the greatest of all his speeches was that which he delivered in Rochester in 1852 on the theme, "What to the Slave is the Fourth of July?" Of abiding significance is the address, "What the Black Man Wants," delivered in the closing year of the war to the Massachusetts Anti-Slavery Society. Only less effective than such efforts as these were the commemorative addresses on Garrison and John Brown. As an orator Douglass was dignified and majestic; he used ringing invective and would not employ humor. In general he insisted that the black man be treated just like any other American, not with sympathy but justice; and he gave to the western world a new sense of the Negro's possibilities.

51. Sojourner Truth and Harriet Tubman.   Two unique characters who came into prominence in the decades just before the Civil War—two of the most remarkable in American history—were Sojourner Truth and Harriet Tubman. Each of these women in her own way did valiant service for the antislavery cause.

The former, originally named Isabella, was untutored, but she had infinite faith and endless resources of wit and wisdom. In 1827, when she should have been free under the emancipating act in New York, and when her master was disposed to retain her services for at least another year, she left early one morning with her youngest child and a little bundle. After some months with an employer who bought her service for the time in question, she went to New York City, where she had some experience with a religious cult in which she was disillusioned. Then there came a day in 1843 when she felt that she could no longer tarry but must go forth on her mission. As to her name she said: "An' the Lord gave me *Sojourner* because I was to travel up an' down the land showin' the people their sins an' bein' a sign unto them. Afterwards I told the Lord I wanted another name, 'cause everybody else had two names; an' the Lord gave me *Truth*, because I was to declare the truth to the people." She lectured wherever she could find a group assembled, and was often entertained in the homes of people of means. Tactful, witty, original, she kept down ridicule, and by her fervor and good sense won many friends. In 1852 she appeared at a woman's suffrage convention in Akron, Ohio, and after some men had spoken slightingly of the purpose of the meeting, routed all opposition with a speech of tremendous power. After the war she helped with relief for the refugees in Washington; and, realizing that the crowding of men to the cities, with the consequent overcrowding of the labor market, would in time increase the criminal element and undermine the physical stamina of the race, she advocated the placing of many of the freedmen on the public lands in the West.[2]

Harriet Tubman was an heroic spirit from Maryland, who not only escaped from bondage herself but later made nineteen trips to the South, helping more than three hundred souls to make their way to freedom. In 1857 she made what was perhaps her most venturesome journey, taking away her aged parents. A tablet in her memory in the Auditorium in Auburn, New York, reads: "With implicit trust in God, she braved every danger and overcame every obstacle. Withal she pos-

[2] For a full account see the recent bright biography by Arthur Huff Fauset, *Sojourner Truth: God's Faithful Pilgrim* (Chapel Hill: The University of North Carolina Press, 1938).

sessed extraordinary foresight and judgment, so that she truthfully said, 'On my underground railroad I nebber run my train off de track and I nebber los' a passenger.' "

52. Story of a Representative Negro. The present chapter has spoken mainly of unusual or gifted characters who in one way or another rendered service and rose to distinction. Perhaps no case that could be cited better illustrates the strivings of the quiet, thrifty, conservative Negro under the system of slavery than that of Lunsford Lane.

This man was a slave belonging to a citizen of Raleigh, North Carolina, and grew up before the era of unusual harshness to slaves which came after the insurrection of Nat Turner. At an early age he learned to read and write, and he gathered much information from the conversation of his master's guests and the speeches of Calhoun and other public men. He once heard a minister say, "It is impossible to enslave an intelligent people," and he never forgot these words.

Earnestly desirous of freedom, he hoarded the fees given him by friends of his master, and by the time he had grown to manhood had saved several hundred dollars. A portion of this money Lane lost in bad investments, and some he spent in special care for his wife, the slave of another master, one Mr. Smith. Having learned from his father the secret of making a superior kind of smoking tobacco, he began to manufacture the product for market, hiring his time for $100 or $120 a year. On the death of his master a few years later, he undertook to purchase his freedom from his mistress, the price agreed upon being $1,000. As a slave, however, he could not make a contract; hence he entrusted the matter to his wife's master. Smith, after making the purchase, asked the court's leave to emancipate Lane, but found that by law a slave could be freed for meritorious service only. The best thing then that Smith could do was to take Lane with him to New York on his next business trip, and have the freedom papers issued there. After this procedure Lane returned a free man to Raleigh, where his business expanded rapidly, as among other things he manufactured pipes and kept a store.

He then undertook to buy his wife and six children. Smith insisted on notes to the amount of $2,500, although eight years before he had bought the wife and two children for $560. Meanwhile Lane was very modest in his attitude toward the white people, dressing as poorly as when a slave and doing nothing that could cause him to be considered an agitator. There were, nevertheless, persons who were jealous of his prosperity, and these called to mind an old act that forbade free Negroes from other states to come to North Carolina. Lane was forced to leave, but he returned after a short while to close up his business. He had paid Smith $560 in cash, and had taken one of his boys to New York. He gave his house and lot for $500 in payment for the freedom of the remainder of his family, undertaking to pay in cash the balance of $1,440. By lecturing in the North, he raised within a year the amount he needed. He then asked the governor of North Carolina for permission to return to the state. The governor replied that he had no authority to grant such permission, but that under the law he thought it would be all right to return, provided the stay was not longer than twenty days. Lane got back to Raleigh on Saturday, April 23, 1842. He spent Sunday with his family, and on Monday went to Smith's store to attend to his business. He was arrested and accused of "delivering abolition lectures in the State of Massachusetts." In court he recounted with simple pathos the whole story of his life, and the case was dismissed. The court house was surrounded by a mob, however, Lane's trunk was searched for abolition literature, and he himself was subjected to other indignities. He was put in jail for safe keeping, and spent the night at the home of an honored citizen, but early the next morning was tarred and feathered. The soldiery at last came to his protection, and he set out with his family for Philadelphia.

Lane's later life was spent in Boston, Worcester, and Oberlin; he had some success in selling a medicine which he made; and he was active in the abolition movement until his death.[3]

[3] See John Spencer Bassett, *Anti-Slavery Leaders of North Carolina* (Baltimore: Johns Hopkins Press, 1902), pp. 60-74.

CHAPTER VI

SLAVERY A NATIONAL ISSUE

53. The Character of the Period. The years from 1820 to 1860 were marked by constant aggression on the part of the slave power. This may be seen from five events of unusual significance: the Missouri Compromise (1820), the annexation of Texas (1845), the Fugitive Slave Law (1850), the Kansas-Nebraska Bill (1854), and the Dred Scott Decision (1857). In addition to these measures in which it succeeded, the South also attempted to acquire Cuba, and it did actually revive the slave trade.

Naturally such aggressiveness did not fail to meet with opposition; in the North arose the Abolitionists, who were uncompromising in their hostility to slavery. The period was thus one of furious controversy, and almost inevitably the country drifted toward war.

54. The Missouri Compromise. Missouri's application in 1818 for entrance into the Union as a slave state resulted in an intense debate lasting two years. In the meantime, in 1819, both Alabama and Maine also applied for admission. Alabama was admitted without much discussion, as she made equal the number of slave and free states. Maine's application, however, brought forth more talk. The Southern men were perfectly willing to consent to admitting it as a free state if Missouri were admitted as a slave state; but the North felt that this would be conceding too much, as Missouri from the first promised to be of unusual importance in the struggle.

At length, largely through the influence of Henry Clay, Congress adopted a compromise whose main provisions were as follows: (1) Maine was to be admitted as a free state; (2) in Missouri there was to be no prohibition of slavery; but (3) slavery was to be prohibited in other states that might be formed out of the Louisiana Purchase north of the line of 36° 30'.

The measure served to allay the strife for some years, but later events proved that the relief was not more than temporary. It was in the debates on the Compromise that the phrase "Mason and Dixon's Line" was first used to indicate the division between the slave and the free states. The line was really only the boundary between Pennsylvania and Maryland drawn (1763-1767) by two English surveyors, Charles Mason and Jeremiah Dixon; but it was now given more popular significance, and it is unfortunate that the phrase should ever have been coined thus to divide the country geographically.

55. **The American Colonization Society. Liberia.** For some decades consideration had been given to the matter of colonizing the Negro at points in Africa, the West Indies, and elsewhere; but it was not until the closing days of 1816 that there was organized in Washington "The American Society for Colonizing the Free People of Color of the United States," commonly known as the American Colonization Society. Of this the president was a southern man; twelve of the seventeen vice-

presidents were southern men; and all of the twelve managers of the project were slaveholders.

Naturally the idea got abroad that the society was organized by slaveholders to perpetuate their institutions by doing away with the free people of color. Early in 1817, in a great mass meeting, the Negroes of Philadelphia denounced the scheme; as prominent a southern man as Robert Y. Hayne showed its expensiveness and futility; and the Abolitionists also opposed it. Yet there were those interested in it who were actuated by the highest of motives. One man in Georgia named Tubman freed his slaves, thirty in all, and placed them in charge of the society with a gift of $10,000.

Settlement on the west coast of Africa was begun early in 1822 and from the first was attended by vicissitudes innumerable. Among the heroic spirits who stood forth in the early years and helped to lay the foundations were Jehudi Ashmun, a young teacher and editor from Vermont who came with a company of freedmen; Elijah Johnson, a colonist who in a dark hour rallied the hearts of his associates; and Lott Cary, a Baptist minister from Richmond, Virginia, who was a colleague of Johnson's in many an effort and a pioneer in mission work. The capital of the new province was named Monrovia, after the president of the United States then in office; and when twenty-five years had passed, on July 26, 1847, the Republic of Liberia issued its declaration of independence and set forth on an independent career. The seal of the republic bore the motto, "The Love of Liberty Brought Us Here."

From that time on sentiment in the United States

began to change. Although at first the Negroes and
their friends had had reason to question the motives
prompting colonization, they were interested in encouraging an independent government, and several young
men received special training for service in Liberia.

56. The Abolitionists. *The Liberator.* The Abolitionists
were those opponents of slavery who, on the ground
that the system was wrong, advocated its instant extinc-
tion without compensation to slave owners. As early
as the second decade of the century, Benjamin Lundy, a
Quaker, advocated abolitionist principles, publishing at
various places a paper, *The Genius of Universal Emancipation.* The movement became aggressive with the
establishment in Boston on January 1, 1831, by William
Lloyd Garrison, of a weekly periodical called *The
Liberator.* In his salutatory editorial Garrison, one of
Lundy's converts, said, "I will be as harsh as truth and
as uncompromising as justice"; and by his arraignment
of the national Constitution he made enemies in the
North as well as in the South.

Prominent also in the movement were Elijah P. Lovejoy, Wendell Phillips, Theodore Parker, John Greenleaf
Whittier, and Lydia Maria Child. Lovejoy, a martyr
if ever there was one, in 1837 lost his life in Alton,
Illinois, while defending himself against the mob attacking the building in which he published an antislavery
paper. Phillips was one of the most polished and forceful
of American orators. Working often against mobs, he
delivered many speeches in behalf of the Negro, one of
the most finished being his address on Toussaint
L'Ouverture. He closed his law office because he would

not swear to support the Constitution; he relinquished
the franchise rather than take any responsibility for a
government that recognized slavery; and he lost sympathy with the Christian church by reason of its
compromising attitude. Theodore Parker, a Unitarian
minister who, like Phillips, was of Massachusetts, inspired many men and women by the courage with
which he applied his religion to current political issues.
Whittier was the poet of the cause. His stirring narrative, "The Slave Ships," set forth the horrors of the
traffic; and "The Farewell" had as its theme the separation of children from their parents. Lydia Maria Child's
*Appeal in Favor of that Class of Americans Called
Africans* (1833) was the first antislavery book published
in the United States.

Representative of the more conservative antislavery
sentiment was William Ellery Channing, New England
idealist and scholar, whose tractate entitled *Slavery*
showed with lofty spirit that the system was out of
harmony with the upward movement of humanity.

The Abolitionists weakened their position by their
refusal to countenance any laws that recognized slavery,
thus repelling many who might otherwise have been
disposed to work with them; but they gained force when
Congress denied them the right of petition and when
President Jackson denied them the use of the mails for
the distribution of their literature. In the South Nat
Turner's insurrection was ascribed to their influence,
though there was no direct connection. In January,
1832, they organized the New England Anti-Slavery
Society, and in December, 1833, the American Anti-

Slavery Society. The more conservative men, those who believed in using the governmental machinery in the work of abolition, organized the Liberty party, which in 1840, and again in 1844, nominated James G. Birney for the presidency. In 1848 the Liberty party became an element of the Free-Soil party, and this in turn was fused in the Republican party in 1854-1856.

57. Southern Sentiment Against Slavery. Not all the antislavery sentiment was to be found in the North. While no one in the South took such radical ground as the Abolitionists (except here and there perhaps a character like the sturdy Cassius Clay of Kentucky), there were many individuals in the section who desired to see the country relieved of slavery.

We have seen that in the Revolutionary era the more prominent patriots were mainly opposed to the system, and that as early as 1778 Virginia attempted to abolish it. The efforts in this state were most prolonged, new attempts being made as late as 1829 and 1831. These would have succeeded if it had not been for the state's unfair system of representation, of which Jefferson complained. In Virginia, however, and North Carolina also, the large slaveowners and planters along the coast had never allowed the "up-country" people, who were largely antislavery in sentiment, a fair share in the government.

In South Carolina, in 1819, with Hayne leading the reform, it was only by a majority of three in the Senate that the state decided not to prohibit the importation of slaves from other states. It seems that the Charleston capitalists, of whom Hayne was the spokesman, desired to check importation not only in order that their own slaves might be more valuable, but also that industries other than cotton and rice production might be started in the state. However selfish the motive, the movement would have had beneficent results, and Hayne was not the only man who could realize the benefit accruing from a well-grounded industrialism.

In general, throughout the South, it was the Scotch-Irish element in the "up-country" that favored the overthrow of slavery in order to gain more political and economic power as well as because of opposition on moral grounds.

58. The Proslavery Argument. While there was some sentiment in the South for the freedom of the slaves or the amelioration of their condition, more and more the dominant thought in this section became crystallized in what was known as the doctrine of States' rights. This term designates those rights of government which a state that has become a member of a federal union may still exercise, and within the sphere of whose activity the central government may not intrude. John C. Calhoun was the foremost expounder of the idea, and the theories of nullification and secession were based upon it.

The South not only endeavored to protect itself thus politically but from time to time through its representative men undertook a comprehensive defense of slavery. T. R. Dew, a professor at William and Mary College, was the foremost apologist for the system. He argued that slavery had advanced the civilization of the world in that it had mitigated the evils of war, had made labor profitable, had changed the nature of savages, and had elevated woman. The slave trade was of course horrible and unjust, but the great advantages of the system more than outweighed the attendant evils. Emancipation and deportation were alike impossible. Even if practicable, they would be inexpedient, for they meant to Virginia the loss of at least a third of her property. Moreover, the system had the advantage of cultivating a republican spirit among the white people. In short, said Dew, in both the economic and the moral point of view, the slaves were "entirely unfit for a state of freedom among the whites." These arguments the Church, with its usual conservatism, supported. It was pointed out that the old Mosaic law recognized slavery, that Jesus Christ did not speak specifically against the system, and that, best of all, the Apostle Paul was on the side of the fugitive slave law, having advised the servant Onesimus to go back to his master Philemon.

Just before the war a distinguished minister in New Orleans, Benjamin M. Palmer, preached a sermon which was printed and spread broadcast throughout the country. He maintained in substance that such an overturning of the established order as the opponents of slavery intended, was not only a violation of the Constitution of the United States, but also the endeavor to bring about nothing less than a reign of anarchy in society.

After the lapse of years the proslavery argument is pitiful in its fallacies, an example of the extremes to which self-interest will sometimes force men of the highest intelligence and honor.

59. Abolition Abroad. In 1833, when the Abolitionists were just becoming aggressive and when the South was fortifying its bulwarks, came the news that England had at last freed the slaves in her colonies. This she had done in a typically English way, paying to the owners £20,000,000 and keeping the slaves under a system of apprenticeship for a term of years. The antislavery forces in America were heartened; Garrison brought an English orator to the United States.

Abolition was making progress in other countries also. Denmark in 1792 had been the first European power to abolish the slave trade. Sweden abolished the traffic in 1813; Holland abolished the trade in 1814 and slavery itself in her colonies in 1846; and Portugal formally forbade the trade in 1836. In 1818 the abolition of the slave trade was effectually accomplished in Santo Domingo, and the independence of the island was formally recognized by France in 1825. The South American countries generally abolished slavery as they emancipated themselves from Spain.

Throughout the period, however, in spite of all of these efforts for reform, there was an illicit traffic in slaves on the high seas, and overtures for an international right of search were constantly made among the great nations. All such efforts were defeated by the defenders of slavery in the United States, and the traffic did not meet with effective resistance until in 1862, under the Lincoln government, a slave trader was hanged. In 1860 the three representative systems of slavery in the New World were those in the United States, in Cuba, and in Brazil.

60. The Annexation of Texas. In 1821 Mexico revolted from Spain. At first she tried an imperial form of government, but in 1824 became a federal republic. Texas, then a part of Mexico, was joined with two other provinces into a state. Here American immigration increased so rapidly that Mexico, becoming alarmed, established military rule and passed antislavery laws. Texas revolted, and an attempt to reduce her to submission resulted in 1836 in her gaining her independence under the lead of General Sam Houston. Independence was followed by a desire for annexation to the United States; but the North was unwilling to approve such an addition to slave territory. In 1844 the question was the leading one in the presidential election, and James K. Polk came into office on a platform pledged to annexation. The Mexican War which followed, growing out of a dispute between Mexico and Texas with reference to the boundary line, was generally regarded in the North as a contest waged in behalf of slavery, and it did much to embitter the sections against each other.

61. The Compromise of 1850. Various new matters now required legislation. Territory in the Southwest other than Texas had been acquired by the Mexican War. In Congress the North sought to enact a bill, known as the Wilmot Proviso, to prohibit slavery in this territory; and the South contended that it should be free from Federal interference. Moreover, California, having acquired a considerable population in a single year as a result of the discovery of gold, was now seeking admission as a free state, without even having been a regularly organized territory.

Accordingly, early in 1850 Henry Clay introduced in the Senate some new compromise resolutions. These were embodied in two bills whose provisions, as finally agreed on, were in substance as follows: (1) California was to be admitted as a free state; (2) Utah and New Mexico were to be organized as territories with no provision as to slavery; (3) the boundaries of Texas were to be fixed practically as they are at present, and $10,-000,000 was to be paid this state for the relinquishment of boundary claims on the nation; (4) the slave trade was to be prohibited in the District of Columbia; and (5) a new and stringent fugitive slave law was to be passed.

Both parties professed to be satisfied, and Henry Clay once more went home beguiled by the fancy that he had saved the Union; but the adjustment was only temporary, and the whole issue was to be reopened just four years later by the trouble in Kansas.

62. The Fugitive Slave Law. The North was especially angered by the Fugitive Slave Law. Gradually the states in that section had succeeded in obstructing the execution of the act of 1793, and in 1842 Pennsylvania definitely decided by a case in court that her officials could not be compelled to aid in the return of runaway slaves.

The new Federal law made possible many grave abuses. It provided for the appointment in each county of a Federal commissioner who was to decide without a jury upon the identity of each supposed fugitive brought before him. He was in no case to accept the word of the fugitive, and when he returned a man he was to receive for his fee twice as much as when he did not return one. The writ for a return, moreover, was to be executed by a United States marshal upon whom a heavy penalty was visited if a slave escaped. Any person could be called to the assistance of a marshal, and anyone who assisted a fugitive was to be heavily punished.

All of this was too much for the Northern states, especially as some persons who had always been free were seized and handed over to slavery.[1] In the years 1854-1860, nine states passed what were known as personal liberty laws. These forbade state officers to assist in the return of alleged fugitives; secured counsel for the fugitives, who were to have the benefit of *habeas corpus* and trial by jury; prohibited the use of state jails for the detention of supposed runaways; and imposed a heavy penalty for the seizure of any free person.

63. **The Underground Railroad** was the name given to the various means by which those in the North who opposed slavery assisted fugitives in escaping from their masters and finding their way to places of safety. By this system hundreds of persons were enabled to get to Canada beyond reach of the enforcement of the Fugitive Slave Law. The most favored routes were through Ohio and Pennsylvania. At various places there were "stations," generally private homes, where the Negroes were kept in garrets or cellars during the day and sent on their way when night came. The work was done at great personal risk, as it was in defiance of the law and as Southern legislatures offered large rewards for the delivery of assistants found below Mason and Dixon's line.

[1] Representative was the experience of Solomon Northup, Negro violinist, of Saratoga Springs, New York, in whose case deception was used to enslave the victim. The story is thrillingly told in *Twelve Years a Slave. Narrative of Solomon Northup, a Citizen of New York, Kidnapped in Washington City in 1841*, first issued in 1853.

The magnitude of the operations may be seen from the fact that for years before the Civil War about 500 Negroes made trips from Canada to the South each year in order to help their friends to escape.

It was in connection with this system that Harriet Tubman did her work, and that many white people in the North suffered in the antislavery cause. Levi Coffin, a Quaker of Newport, Indiana, was commonly considered the head of the enterprise. Once being asked under oath if he had aided slaves, he replied that he had no legal knowledge of having done so. He had ministered, it was true, to certain destitute persons who told him that they had been slaves; but he had only their word for it, and as the word of a slave could not be received in court, he could not reasonably be considered guilty. He was released, but everybody did not fare so well. Ruth Shore, of Sandusky, Ohio, paid in fines for assisting runaway slaves a total of $3,000. Thomas Garrett paid $8,000, and Calvin Fairbank served seventeen years in the penitentiary. In spite of legal pressure, however, the work went on. An investigator of the subject, Wilbur H. Siebert, names 3,211 "agents, station keepers, and conductors." Coffin received annually in his house about 100 fugitives, and Garrett helped as many as 2,700 to escape.

64. Renewal of the Slave Trade. The response of the South to the operation of Underground Railroad was practically a reopening of the slave trade. We have seen that the first national act against the trade was passed in 1794 and that the traffic was nominally abolished in 1807. There was no adequate machinery for enforcement, however, and before long the government was aware that an illicit trade was being carried on. Through such inlets as those near the ports of Galveston and Fernandina, slaves were smuggled in, sometimes in great numbers. From 1820 to 1840, by reason of a repressive measure of 1819, the traffic declined greatly. Meanwhile, however, the development of the cotton industry in the South led to a demand for more land and more slaves. The desire for land accounted for the annexation of Texas, and that for more slaves was for some time satisfied by importations from Virginia and Maryland, which states now became joined to the far South by the close tie of economic interest. Thus matters drifted until 1850, and it was in the decade that followed that the traffic on the high seas was so greatly renewed. It became more and more open and defiant until, as Stephen A. Douglas computed, as many as 15,000 slaves were brought into the country in 1859. The feeling of many in the South was voiced in a resolution offered in a commercial convention in Vicksburg to the effect that "all laws, State or Federal, prohibiting the African slave trade, ought to be repealed."

65. The Kansas-Nebraska Bill. The point of the Kansas-Nebraska Bill of 1854 is very simple; this measure in substance repealed the provisions of the Missouri Compromise in the interest of the slave power. It was promoted by Stephen A. Douglas, chairman of the Senate Committee on Territories, who contended that the Compromise of 1850, in giving territories the right of option as to slavery, had already annulled the Missouri Compromise. This construction was embodied in the bill

for the organization of the territories of Kansas and Nebraska with limits much larger than those of the present states with these names. There was provision for "squatter sovereignty," the theory that the people in any territory should be free to regulate their domestic institutions in their own way subject only to the Constitution of the United States. The North felt outraged by the bill, and immediately began to form the Republican party.

66. The Origin of the Republican Party. The new Republican party differed from the Liberty and Free-Soil parties that had preceded it in that it was not a minor organization but one that so commanded the support of adherents as to be able to play a major role in the nation's affairs. The old Whig party had been uncertain in principle, and some men, notably Frederick Douglass and William Lloyd Garrison, felt at first that even the new organization was not sufficiently radical in its opposition to slavery. Before long, however, all elements working for freedom, both radical and conservative, found in the Republican party the best means of presenting a united front. They realized that not only the freedom of the Negro was at stake, but also the larger economic development of the country, the future of labor, and public education.

In 1856 the Republicans put forth as their candidate for the presidency John C. Frémont, and he was defeated by Buchanan. Four years later they nominated Abraham Lincoln, and with him were successful. Many young men in the North were inspired by a new hope for the future of democracy. On the other hand the slavery group realized that it would not longer be permitted to dominate the life of the country, and within a few weeks of the election of Lincoln the movement for secession began.

67. The Anthony Burns Incident.   Opposition to the Kansas-Nebraska Bill was shown not only by the organization of the Republican party but also by incidents in different communities. The first demonstration took place in Boston.

Anthony Burns was a slave who had escaped from Virginia and was at work in Boston in the winter of 1853-1854. He was discovered by a United States marshal who presented a writ for his arrest. Public feeling was immediately aroused. Wendell Phillips and Theodore Parker delivered strong addresses at a meeting in Faneuil Hall while an unsuccessful attempt to rescue Burns from the Court House was made under the leadership of Thomas W. Higginson, who, with others of the attacking party, was wounded. It was finally decided in court that Burns must be returned to his master. The law was obeyed; but Boston had been made very angry, and generally her feeling had counted for something in the history of the country. The people draped their houses in mourning and hissed the procession that took Burns to his ship. This incident did more to crystallize Northern sentiment against slavery than any other except the exploit of John Brown, and this was the last time that a fugitive slave was taken from Boston. Burns was afterwards bought from his master by popular subscription. He became a citizen of Boston and later a Baptist minister in Canada.

68. The Dred Scott Decision. One further act was yet to fill the cup of bitterness in the North to the brim. In 1834 Dr. Emerson, an army officer stationed in Missouri, removed to Illinois, taking with him his slave, Dred Scott. Two years later, again accompanied by Scott, he went to Minnesota. In Illinois slavery was prohibited by state law, and Minnesota was a free territory. In 1838 Emerson returned with Scott to Missouri. After a while the slave raised the important question, Had not his residence outside of a slave state made him a free man? When beaten by his master in 1848, Scott with the aid of antislavery lawyers brought a suit against him for assault and battery, and the circuit court of St. Louis rendered a decision in the Negro's favor. Emerson appealed, and in 1852 the supreme court of the state reversed the decision of the lower court. Not long thereafter Emerson sold Scott to a citizen of New York named Sandford. Scott now brought suit against Sandford, on the ground that they were citizens of different states. The case finally reached the Supreme Court of the United States, which in 1857 handed down the decision that Scott was not a citizen of Missouri and had no standing in the Federal courts, that a slave was only a piece of property, and that a master might take his property to any place he chose within the jurisdiction of the United States. The ownership of Scott and his family soon passed to a Massachusetts family by whom they were liberated; but the important decision that his case had called forth aroused the most intense excitement throughout the country.

69. *Uncle Tom's Cabin.* In the year 1852 appeared a book that had an amazing sale and that made a peculiar appeal to the heart of the country. For some years Harriet Beecher Stowe, wife of a theological professor, had lived with her husband in Cincinnati. There she was close to the system of slavery and saw much of its actual working. In 1850 Professor Stowe accepted a position in Bowdoin College, Brunswick, Maine, and removed his family thither. Here in the form of a story, with the title *Uncle Tom's Cabin*, Mrs. Stowe brought together her observations on slavery, first as a serial and then as a book.

What the work lacked in literary finish it more than made up in human interest. Here was Uncle Tom himself, embodiment of all that was pious and forbearing. Here too were little Eva, a spirit of light in the world about her; her father, the over-indulgent and improvident master; Aunt Ophelia from New England, to whom the whole South was shiftless; Cassy, the slave darling fallen on evil days; Simon Legree, the worst type of plantation slaveowner; and George Harris, the ambitious spirit longing to break its bonds.

Many people criticised the portrayal as overdrawn, and the South felt itself misrepresented. Accordingly in 1853 Mrs. Stowe published *A Key to Uncle Tom's Cabin*, setting forth the facts and documents used in the story, and showing, among other things, that the prototype of Uncle Tom was Josiah Henson, a Negro who, born a slave in Maryland, in early manhood made his escape to Canada.

The author wrote many other books, but, with the

exception of *Dred*, a story ominous with impending disaster, they all pale into insignificance by the side of her great success. *Uncle Tom's Cabin* alone, however, was strong enough for a lifework, and even today it is sometimes presented on the stage.

70. Henry Ward Beecher. Of only less service to the cause of the slave than Mrs. Stowe was her brother, Henry Ward Beecher. This remarkable preacher, by his bold support of reforms, made his large and intelligent congregation at Plymouth Church, Brooklyn, one of the most famous in the world. He was untiring in his support of the antislavery cause and on one occasion appealed to his audience by bringing a slave girl into his pulpit and asking for the price of her ransom. In 1863 he delivered in England a series of addresses before audiences largely hostile. As the industry of England was largely dependent on the supply of cotton from the Southern states, opinion in that country was strongly divided; and Beecher not only impressed thousands by his courage but also did much to win favor for the North.

71. Charles Sumner. What Beecher was in the pulpit, and Wendell Phillips was on the public platform, Charles Sumner was in the United State Senate. This scholarly statesman came into prominence in 1845 by a Fourth-of-July oration denouncing war. In 1851 he was sent to the Senate, of which he was a member until his death in 1874. Though not an Abolitionist, he became the leader of the antislavery forces, and by his powerful opposition to the Kansas-Nebraska Bill he incurred the hatred of the South, receiving many threats of personal violence. In 1856, in fact, while working at his desk in the Senate chamber, he was severely assaulted with a cane by Preston S. Brooks, of South Carolina. The attack greatly embittered the North. Sumner was forced to retire temporarily from public life and never fully recovered As early as 1864 he formulated what was known as the "state suicide" theory with reference to the seceded states, and he became the leader of the opposition to President Johnson's plan of reconstruction. It was due to him more than anyone else that the principle of suffrage, irrespective of race or color, was given formal statement in the national Constitution.

72. *The Impending Crisis.* While leaders in the North were thus opposing slavery mainly on moral or political grounds, it remained for a son of the South, a representative of white men of limited means, to make a very different attack. *The Impending Crisis of the South*, produced four years before the Civil War, was surpassed in sensational interest by no book of the period except *Uncle Tom's Cabin*. The author, Hinton Rowan Helper, was from North Carolina. He did not place himself upon the broadest principles of statesmanship; he had little interest in the Negro slave as such; and the great planters of the South were to him the "whelps" and "curs" of slavery. Speaking simply as the voice of nonslaveholding white men of the South, he set forth such unpleasant truths as that the real and personal property, including slaves, of Virginia, North Carolina, Tennessee, Missouri, Arkansas, Florida, and Texas, taken all together, was less than the real and personal property in the single state of New York; that the hay crop alone of the North was worth more than all the cotton, rice, tobacco, hay, hemp, and cane sugar of the South; that representation in Southern legislatures was unfair; that in Congress a Southern planter was twice as powerful as a Northern man; that slavery was to blame for the migration from the South to the West; and that in short the system was harmful in its influence in every way.

Property owners in the South did not care to hear such things; Helper's book was proscribed, and the author himself found it more advisable to live in New York than in North Carolina. *The Impending Crisis* was eagerly read, however, and it succeeded as a book because it attacked with some degree of honesty a great economic problem.

73. John Brown. For forty years slavery had been the most important subject before the American people. Garrison had been persecuted, Lovejoy had been killed, Phillips and Douglass had talked, slaves had escaped to Canada, and Mrs. Stowe had written a powerful book; still slavery had gone on its masterful career, seemingly invincible. At last the situation had become so inflammable that only a spark was needed to send the country into flame.

That spark was supplied by John Brown. This man was born in Connecticut in 1800. In his earlier years he made various experiments in business, in all of which he was unsuccessful. In 1855 he joined five of his sons in Kansas, where the opponents and the advocates of slavery were fiercely arrayed against each other. Here, as Phillips said, he actually began life. Working with the radical antislavery men, he took the lead in the massacre of five of his opponents at Pottawatomie on May 24,

1856. Later in the year, at Ossawatomie, he attracted national attention by the energy with which he repelled an invading force from Missouri. All of this was in line with his conviction that, as slavery was unholy, he was justified in killing slaveholders. The memorable deed of his life occurred in 1859. He conceived a plan to seize some strong position in the mountains of Virginia, whence he might sally forth and make the slave power insecure. In pursuance of his plan, he engaged a farm near his objective point, and on October 16, with nineteen assistants, five of whom were Negroes, he surprised and captured the arsenal at Harpers Ferry. Two days later, after being wounded, he was captured by United States troops under the command of Robert E. Lee. He was convicted of treason and murder, and hanged December 2.

John Brown's exploit made a profound impression on the country, and he has since been the subject of most conflicting opinion. Some think of him as a fanatic who committed a criminal deed, while to others he was a man of noble purpose borne by the intensity of his convictions into martyrdom.

74. Secession.   In their nominating convention of 1860 the Democrats were hopelessly divided, and thus the way was made easier for the election of the Republican candidate, Abraham Lincoln. Within a few weeks the secession of the Southern states followed. South Carolina led with an ordinance of December 20, 1860, and the other states acted in their conventions early in the next year.

That opinion was not unanimous for secession may be seen from the contest in Georgia. In the preliminary vote on the right or duty of withdrawal there were 165 in favor and 130 who opposed; and the final vote on secession itself was 208 to 89.

Delegates from the different states organized in Montgomery, Alabama, the Provisional Government of the Confederate States of America, although Richmond, Virginia, later became the capital. Jefferson Davis, who had served in the cabinet of President Pierce as Secretary of War, and who had just resigned as United States Senator from Mississippi, was elected president; and the vice-president was Alexander H. Stephens, who had made in the Georgia legislature the strongest speech against secession.

Once the great step of withdrawal from the Union had been taken, the South was not disposed to entrust its fortunes to those who were known as "fire-eaters"; and, as Professor William E. Dodd [2] has said, the new government presented the amazing spectacle of a revolution led by its opponents.

The Confederacy itself, moreover, was founded on a fallacy. A central government either had authority to enforce its decrees or it had not. If it had authority, then the North was right in its position. If it had not authority, then such a government was useless. It developed that the Confederacy had not the necessary authority.

[2] Dr. William E. Dodd, formerly Professor of American History at the University of Chicago, authority on the history of the South, author of *Expansion and Conflict* (Boston: Houghton Mifflin Co., 1915) and other books dealing with the Civil War.

In the heat of the moment, however, this innate weakness was not perceived, and organization went forward.

On April 12 General Beauregard fired on Fort Sumter in Charleston harbor, and the Civil War had begun.

CHAPTER VII

SOCIAL PROGRESS BEFORE THE CIVIL WAR

75. The Problem Beyond Slavery. It has already been suggested that the problem with which the country was wrestling far transcended the subject of slavery. In the last analysis in fact, slavery was merely an incident—a temporary status into which some people from a foreign land happened to fall, and from which they were destined to be delivered. The larger question was, what was to be the final place in the American body politic of those who for the time being were in bondage? In the answering of this, importance attached to the Negro himself; but the question was not limited to a single race. Ultimately it was the destiny of the United States that was to be considered, and all the ideals on which the country was based came to the testing. If this was indeed a democratic government, deriving its just powers from the consent of the governed, then it could not overlook the challenge of a group that struggled with oppression.

76. The Field of Improvement. In a previous chapter we studied the Negro's reaction to the system of slavery, and we saw that his effort to deliver himself embraced means as different as insurrection and colonization. If, however, slavery was to be only a temporary status, and if the Negro was to find a place with other racial elements in the life of the United States, we are driven to a further question. With all of the disabilities, and in spite of them, to what extent by 1860 had he advanced in culture and citizenship? What was he doing on his own account to rise to the full stature of manhood? Naturally in the answer to this we shall have to be concerned primarily with people who had attained nominal freedom. In 1860 the free persons formed just one ninth of the total Negro population of the country, there being 487,970 of them in comparison to 3,953,760 slaves. It is worthy of note that, in spite of all the disadvantages they faced, these free Negroes had entered every large field of endeavor in which the race is at work today.

77. Representative Negro Views. From the first the possibility and the danger of an *imperium in imperio* were perceived, and it is worth while to note the views of two or three outstanding Negro men. James W. C. Pennington, undoubtedly a leader, said in his lectures in London and Glasgow: "The colored population of the United States have no destiny separate from that of the nation in which they form an integral part. Our destiny is bound up with that of America. Her ship is ours; her pilot is ours; her storms are ours; her calms are ours. If she breaks upon any rock, we break with her. If we, born in America, can not live upon the same soil upon terms of equality with the descendants of Scotchmen, Englishmen, Irishmen, Frenchmen, Germans, Hungarians, Greeks, and Poles, then the fundamental theory of America fails and falls to the ground." [1]

While Negro men were in agreement on this funda-

---

[1] William C. Nell, *The Colored Patriots of the American Revolution* (Boston: R. F. Wallcut, 1855), p. 356.

mental matter, more and more there developed two lines of thought, equally honest, as to the means by which the race itself could advance. The leader of one school of thought was Richard Allen, first bishop of the African Methodist Episcopal Church. When this man and his friends found that in white churches they were not treated with courtesy, they determined to have their own church, their own bishop, and to build up their own enterprises in any line whatsoever. The foremost representative of the opposing line of thought was Frederick Douglass, who deprecated the idea of separate places of worship, feeling that his people should join such societies as did not regard color as a test of membership. There is more difference between these two positions than can be accounted for by the lapse of forty years between the height of the work of Allen and that of Douglass. Allen certainly did not approve segregation under the law, and no man worked harder than he to relieve his people from proscription. Douglass, on the other hand, who did not formally countenance racial organizations, again and again presided over gatherings of Negro men. In the last analysis, however, it was Allen who laid the basis of distinctively Negro enterprise, and Douglass who felt that it was best for the race to lose itself as quickly as possible in the general body politic.

78. The Church. From the first the church was the Negro's foremost form of social organization, and in the years just before the Civil War the growth that had begun several decades before continued.

Scattered Baptist churches were most numerous, and

Lott Cary, a minister of this group, as we have seen, became a pioneer in mission work in Africa.

The African Methodist Episcopal denomination advanced from 7 churches and 400 members in 1816 to 286 churches and 73,000 members at the close of the war. Naturally such a distinctively Negro organization could make little progress in the South as long as slavery flourished, but there were visits to this field, and Bishop William Paul Quinn blazed a path in the West, going from Pittsburgh to St. Louis.

Of denominations other than the Baptist and the Methodist, the most prominent in the earlier years was the Presbyterian, whose first Negro ministers were John Gloucester and John Chavis. Gloucester owed his training to the liberal tendencies that about 1800 were still strong in eastern Tennessee and Kentucky, and in 1810 took charge of the African Presbyterian Church that three years before had been established in Philadelphia. He had a rich musical voice and led a dignified life, and four sons of his also became Presbyterian ministers. Chavis had a very unusual career. After passing through a regular course of academic studies at Washington Academy, now Washington and Lee University, in 1801 he was commissioned by the General Assembly of the Presbyterians as a missionary to the Negroes. He worked with increasing reputation not only as a minister but also as a teacher of children, both white and colored, until Nat Turner's insurrection caused the North Carolina legislature to pass an act silencing all Negro preachers.

In the earlier years of the century, before social conditions were so fixed as they later became, a few men of Negro descent were pastors of white congregations. Lemuel Haynes (1753-1833), the first man of color formally ordained in the United States and a speaker of unusual spiritual power, so served several Congregational churches in New England, spending the last eleven years of his life in Granville, New York. About the middle of the century Samuel Ringgold Ward, author of the *Autobiography of a Fugitive Negro* and one of the most eloquent men of the time, was for several years pastor of a white Congregational church in Courtlandville, New York.

79. The Professions. The Negro was advancing not only in the church, but also in the professions of law and medicine. Before the Civil War not less than five men of Negro descent were admitted to the bar in Massachusetts, and of these Robert Morris, Jr., seems to have been the most able. In the earlier years of the century James Derham, of New Orleans, became the first recognized Negro physician of whom there is a complete record. Born in Philadelphia in 1762, he was transferred while still a boy as slave to a physician for whom he learned to perform minor duties. Afterward he was sold to a physician in New Orleans, who used him as an assistant. He won his freedom, became familiar with French and Spanish as well as English, and in time commanded general respect by his learning and skill. In New York, as we have seen, about the middle of the century, James McCune Smith, a graduate of the University of Glasgow, was prominent. He was the author of several scientific papers, a man of wide interests, and universally held in high esteem. Several young men received training under the auspices of the American Colonization Society. Among these were John V. De Grasse, of New York, and Thomas J. White, of Brooklyn, who completed the medical course at Bowdoin in 1849.

80. Fraternal Organizations. We have already observed the beginning of Negro Masonry in 1787 under the leadership of Prince Hall. In 1847 the Prince Hall Lodge in Massachusetts, the First Independent African Grand Lodge in Pennsylvania, and the Hiram Grand Lodge of Pennsylvania formed a National Grand Lodge, and from one or another of these all other Grand Lodges of Negro Masons have descended.

In 1842 the members of the Philomathean Institute of New York and of the Philadelphia Library Company and Debating Society applied for admission to the International Order of Odd Fellows. They were refused on account of their race. Thereupon Peter Ogden, a Negro, who served as a steward on vessels crossing the Atlantic, and who had joined the Grand United Order of Odd Fellows of England, applied to his organization in behalf of his friends in the United States. In October, 1842, accordingly, charter was thus secured for the first Negro American lodge, Philomathean, No. 646, of New York, and this was duly set up March 1, 1843, James McCune Smith being the first secretary. It was followed within the next two years by lodges in New York, Philadelphia, Albany, and Poughkeepsie.

The Knights of Pythias were not organized until

1864, but the Grand Order of Galilean Fisherman started on its career in Baltimore in 1856.

To some extent these organizations took the place of clubs, and their meetings were relished accordingly; but they also partook of the features of what were known as benefit societies. These were first confined to small groups of persons well known to one another, thus being genuinely fraternal. They imposed an initiation fee and monthly dues, and gave help in sickness, with the guarantee of payment of one's funeral expenses and subsequent help to his widow. By 1838 there were in Philadelphia alone 100 such groups with 7,448 members. In general the benefit societies anticipated our modern insurance companies.

81. Civil Rights.   In the sphere of civil rights the Negroes, in spite of circumstances, were making progress, and that by their own efforts as well as those of their friends the Abolitionists.

Largely through the tradition established by Paul Cuffe, New Bedford, Massachusetts, was prominent in all that made for racial advance. In that city by 1850 the Negro voters held the balance of power and thus exerted a potent influence on election days.[2] In 1840 there was repealed so much of the Massachusetts statutes as forbade intermarriage between the races "contrary to the principles of Christianity and republicanism." In the same state, a little more than two years later, an act forbidding discrimination on railroads was passed.

In New York City an interesting case arose over public conveyances. When, about 1852, horsecars began to

[2] Nell, *The Colored Patriots of the American Revolution*, p. 111.

supersede omnibuses on the streets, the Negro was excluded from the use of them; and he continued to be excluded even after a court decision gave him the right to enter. One Sunday in May, 1855, however, James W. C. Pennington, after service, reminded his hearers of the decision in court, urged them to stand up for their rights, and especially to inform their friends coming for an anniversary that the law was with them. He himself then boarded a car on Sixth Avenue, refused to leave when ordered to do so, and was forcibly ejected. He brought suit against the company and won his case; and thus the Negro made further advance toward full citizenship in New York.[3]

82. Journalism. In the effort that was made for civil rights the periodicals that had been started helped decidedly.

In March, 1827, appeared the first number of *The Journal of Freedom* (commonly known as *Freedom's Journal*), a weekly edited by Samuel E. Cornish, a Presbyterian minister, and John B. Russwurm, soon to be a graduate of Bowdoin. Support was inadequate, and the two editors differed on the matter of colonization. In the issue for September 5, 1827, Russwurm supported the idea, and Cornish resigned the next week. Russwurm continued in charge until February, 1829, when he left to become Superintendent of Education in Liberia. Cornish now assumed sole charge and for twenty months issued the periodical under the name *Rights for All*. In

[3] John Bach McMaster, *A History of the People of the United States, from the Revolution to the Civil War* (New York: D. Appleton & Co., 1883-1913), VIII, 74.

1841 he became the first of the editors of the *Colored American*, a paper that lasted for four years.

There were several other early periodicals, but of more than usual importance was *The North Star*, which Douglass began to issue in Rochester in 1847, the name being changed three years later to *Frederick Douglass' Paper*.

Outstanding among the magazines was the *Anglo-African*, which began publication in New York in January, 1859, and appeared regularly for fifteen months. The editor, Thomas Hamilton, was not able to pay for articles, but even so he secured as contributors some of the most prominent Negroes of the day, among them being James McCune Smith, Martin R. Delany, Alexander Crummell, and Edward W. Blyden.

83. **Business Enterprise.** Economic progress before 1860 was far more than is sometimes supposed. In spite of the fact that many doors in the North and West were closed, and that white artisans were often hostile, there was distinct advance in many fields. For decades the South had depended upon Negro labor in the trades. Many brick masons, carpenters, and shoemakers became highly efficient; and when some of the more enterprising went to other sections, they took their training with them. In 1852, of 3,500 Negroes in Cincinnati, 200 were holders of property and taxpayers. Among 1,696 Negroes at work in Philadelphia in 1856, there were 615 tailors, dressmakers, and shirtmakers, 248 barbers, 66 shoemakers, 53 brickmakers, 49 carpenters, 45 milliners, 24 tanners, 22 blacksmiths, and 22 cake bakers or con-

fectioners. There were also 16 school teachers, 15 musicians, and 6 physicians at work in the city.[4]

The foremost man of business in the race about 1850 was Stephen Smith, of the firm of Smith and Whipper, of Columbia, Pennsylvania,[5] a lumber merchant, engaged in real estate in Philadelphia, where he owned more than fifty brick houses. Henry Boyd, of Cincinnati, was the proprietor of a bedstead manufactory that sometimes employed as many as twenty-five men. Several caterers and tailors became known as having the best places in their line of business in their respective cities. John Julius, of Pittsburgh, was the proprietor of a brilliant place called Concert Hall. It was here that a reception was held in 1840 for President-elect William Henry Harrison. Cordovell became widely known as the name of the leading tailor and designer of fashions in New Orleans.

84. "Free Men of Color." Cordovell was representative of a special group in the South, those people of mixed blood who were sometimes descended from the early French or Spanish settlers. In Louisiana the F. M. C. (Free Man of Color) held a distinct and anomalous place in society.[6] As a free man he had certain rights, and sometimes his property holdings were large. In New Orleans a few years before the Civil War not less than

[4] Benjamin C. Bacon, *Statistics of the Colored People of Philadelphia* (Philadelphia: T. E. Chapman, 1856), pp. 13-14.

[5] Martin R. Delany, *The Condition, Elevation, Emigration, and Destiny of Colored People of the United States, Politically Considered* (Philadelphia, 1852).

[6] See P. F. de Gournay, "The F. M. C.'s of Louisiana," *Lippincott's Magazine*, April, 1894; and Calvin Dill Wilson, "Black Masters," *North American Review*, November, 1905.

one fifth of the taxable property was in the hands of those in the group. At the same time the lot of these people was one of endless humiliation. They were often compelled to have papers filled out by white guardians, and when the name of a free man of color appeared on any legal document, the initials F. M. C. had to be appended. They were not allowed to have any companionship with slaves.

Sometimes free colored men owned their women and children in order that the latter might escape the law against Negroes recently emancipated; or the situation was sometimes reversed, as in Norfolk, Va., where several women owned their husbands. In Louisiana these people petitioned in vain for the suffrage, and at the outbreak of the Civil War organized and equipped for the Confederacy two battalions of five hundred men. For these they chose two distinguished white commanders, and the governor accepted their services, only to have to inform them later that the Confederacy objected to the enrolling of Negro men.

In general the F. M. C.'s were industrious and they almost monopolized one or two avenues of employment. As was perhaps natural, they did not have the deepest sympathy with the Negro still in bondage. Some of them sent their children to France to be educated, and sometimes they themselves left never to return.

85. Education.   In spite of the disadvantages they had to meet, the Negro people also made general advance in education.

Even in the South, where it was against the law, some persons received teaching through private or clandestine sources.[7] More than one slave learned the alphabet while amusing the son of his master. In Charleston for some years before the Civil War free Negroes could attend schools specially designed for their benefit, and the course of study not infrequently embraced such subjects as physiology, physics, and plane geometry. In 1835, and again after John Brown's raid, there were repressive measures. These were not always fully enforced, but at the outbreak of the war schools were closed altogether.

In the North, though there was some proscription, conditions in general were much better. As early as 1850 there were in the public schools of New York 3,393 Negro children, and the proportion to the total Negro population was about the same as that of white children to the total white population. Two institutions for the higher education of the Negro were established before the war, Lincoln University in Pennsylvania in 1854 and Wilberforce in Ohio in 1856. Oberlin, moreover, was founded in 1833. In 1835 an Abolitionist, Asa Mahan, of Lane Seminary, was offered the presidency. He said that he would accept only if Negroes were admitted on equal terms with other students, and after a warm debate, the trustees voted in his favor. Though, before this, individual Negroes had found their way into Northern institutions, it was here at Oberlin that they first received a genuine welcome. By 1860 nearly one third of the students were of the Negro race, and one

[7] For interesting examples, see Carter G. Woodson, *The Education of the Negro Prior to 1861* (New York: G. P. Putnam's Sons, 1915).

of the graduates, John M. Langston, was soon to be distinguished in the life of his people and of the country.

86. Invention. Before 1860 a situation that arose more than once took from Negroes the real credit for inventions. If a slave perfected an original device, he was not permitted to take out a patent, for no slave could make a contract. At the same time his master could not take out the patent for him, as the Government would not recognize the right of the slave to make assignment. Negroes, who did most of the mechanical work in the South before the Civil War, made more than one suggestion for the improvement of machinery. We have already referred to the claim put forth by a member of the race for the real credit of the cotton gin. The honor of being the first Negro to be granted a patent belongs to Henry Blair, of Maryland, who in 1834 received official protection for his invention of a corn harvester.

87. Literature. Much was attempted in the field of literature, though little was produced that was definitive.

Importance attaches to a group of narratives written by those who had had experience with slavery. One of the most notable was that of Frederick Douglass, revised and enlarged in 1855 as *My Bondage and My Freedom*. Similarly, the first account by Josiah Henson, the original of Uncle Tom, was enlarged and reissued as *Truth Stranger than Fiction: Father Henson's Story of His Own Life* (1858). Douglass and Henson each brought out his story later in a third form. Hardly anything was more interesting than Samuel Northup's *Twelve Years a Slave* (1853), the story of a player on the violin who was enticed away from his home in Saratoga Springs, New York, to join a circus, and later awoke to find himself a slave in Washington.

The most prolific author of the period was William Wells Brown, who not only wrote a narrative but also attempted various things in history, fiction, and the drama. With his novel *Clotel, or The President's Daughter* (London, 1853, the American edition, 1864, being entitled *Clotelle: A Tale of the Southern States*), and his play in five acts, *The Escape* (1858), he must be given the credit of being a pioneer; but he had neither the training nor the temperament of a finished literary worker.

Several men issued booklets of verse. One of the most interesting of the writers was George M. Horton, slave poet of Chapel Hill, who, beginning with *The Hope of Liberty* (1829), later showed that he had an original vein of humor. Intense and clear in its exposition of wrong was a very small book, *America, and Other Poems* (1853), the work of James M. Whitfield, a young man who died early.

Alexander Crummell, who excelled in the essay, and Frances E. W. Harper, lecturer and writer of popular verse, both appeared on the scene, but it was in the next generation that the career of each came to full fruition.

88. **The Stage, Music, and Art.** On the stage, in music, and in art there were at least one or two performers who could lay claim to eminence in each field.

Ira Aldridge, who as a young man became acquainted with the great English actor, Edmund Kean, later achieved extraordinary success on the stage in the capitals of Europe. A man of superb presence, he was especially thrilling in the part of Othello, and he received tokens of esteem from the sovereigns of three or four different countries.

Frank Johnson, of Philadelphia, developed a band that won the favor of Queen Victoria. Justin Holland, who became a teacher of music in Cleveland, studied comprehensively the playing of the guitar, on which subject he later wrote a book. Richard Lambert, a free man of color and a teacher of music in New Orleans, had two sons, Lucien and Sidney, both of whom became distinguished pianists. Lucien Lambert, after studying in Paris, went to Brazil, where he became a manufacturer of pianos; and Sidney became a composer and teacher in Paris. The outstanding singer of the period was Elizabeth Taylor Greenfield, of Philadelphia, who had a voice embracing twenty-seven notes, said by one paper to reach "from the sonorous bass of a baritone to a few notes above even Jenny Lind's highest." Prominent among the men was Thomas J. Bowers, a tenor of handsome countenance and fine stage presence.

Patrick Reason, of New York, was engaged by Abolitionists to engrave the frontispieces of several biographies of former slaves, and he did much other work as well. Daniel Warbourg, a free man of color in New Orleans, was also an engraver. His brother, Eugene Warbourg, a sculptor, made a reputation in Europe. Outstanding among the painters of the era was Robert Duncanson, who received part of his training in Europe, and whose landscapes are today preserved in New York, Philadelphia, and Cincinnati.

CHAPTER VIII

EMANCIPATION

89. Steps Leading to the Proclamation. At the outbreak of the Civil War two great questions affecting the Negro overshadowed all others, those of his freedom and of his employment as a soldier. There was a demand from antislavery sources that President Lincoln dispose of the first immediately. He, however, did not feel that he should act hastily. Sentiment in the North was not united; and in 1862 the Confederates, with brilliant generalship, were winning some of their greatest victories. The repulse of Lee at Antietam at length gave the President the opportunity for which he had waited, and he now felt that he could act with grace to the Northern arms. Accordingly on September 22, 1862, he issued a preliminary declaration giving notice that on January 1, 1863, he would free the slaves in the states still in rebellion, and asserting as before that the object of the war was the preservation of the Union.

90. The Emancipation Proclamation. The Proclamation as finally issued on January 1, 1863, is one of the most important public documents in the history of the United States, ranking only below the Declaration of Independence and the Constitution itself. Its full text is as follows:

Whereas, on the twenty-second day of September, in the year of our Lord one thousand eight hundred and sixty-two, a proclamation was issued by the President of the United States, containing among other things, the following, to wit:

"That on the first day of January, in the year of our Lord one thousand eight hundred and sixty-three, all persons held as slaves within any state or designated part of a state, the people whereof shall then be in rebellion against the United States, shall be then, thenceforward, and forever free; and the executive government of the United States, including the military and naval authority thereof, will recognize and maintain the freedom of such persons, and will do no act or acts to repress such persons, or any of them, in any efforts they may make for their actual freedom.

"That the Executive will, on the first day of January aforesaid, by proclamation, designate the states and parts of states, if any, in which the people thereof shall then be in rebellion against the United States; and the fact that any state, or the people thereof, shall on that day be in good faith represented in the Congress of the United States, by members chosen thereto at elections wherein a majority of the qualified voters of such state shall have participated, shall, in the absence of strong countervailing testimony, be deemed conclusive evidence that such state, and the people thereof, are not then in rebellion against the United States."

Now, therefore, I, ABRAHAM LINCOLN, President of the United States, by virtue of the power in me vested as Commander-in-Chief of the Army and Navy of the United States, in time of actual armed rebellion against the authority and government of the United States, and as a fit and necessary war measure for suppressing said rebellion, do on this first day of January, in the year of our Lord one thousand eight hundred and sixty-three, and in accordance with my purpose so to do, publicly proclaimed for the full period of one hundred days from the date first above mentioned, order and designate as the states and parts of states wherein the people thereof respectively are this day in rebellion against the United States, the following to wit:

Arkansas, Texas, Louisiana (except the parishes of St. Bernard, Plaquemines, Jefferson, St. John, St. Charles, St. James, Ascension, Assumption, Terre Bonne, Lafourche, St. Marie, St. Martin, and Orleans, including the city of New Orleans), Mississippi, Alabama, Florida, Georgia, South Carolina, North Carolina, and Virginia (except the forty-eight counties designated as West Virginia, and also the counties of Berkeley, Accomac, Northampton, Elizabeth City, York, Princess Anne, and Norfolk, including the cities of Norfolk and Portsmouth), and which excepted parts are, for the present, left precisely as if this proclamation were not issued.

And by virtue of the power and for the purpose aforesaid, I do order and declare that all persons held as slaves within said designated states and parts of states are and henceforward shall be free, and that the executive government of the United States, including the military and naval authorities thereof, will recognize and maintain the freedom of said persons.

And I hereby enjoin upon the people so declared to be free to abstain from all violence, unless in necessary self-defense; and I recommend to them that, in all cases when allowed, they labor faithfully for reasonable wages.

And I further declare and make known that such persons, of suitable condition, will be received into the armed service of the United States, to garrison forts, positions, stations, and other places, and to man vessels of all sorts in said service.

And upon this act, sincerely believed to be an act of justice, warranted by the Constitution upon military necessity, I invoke the considerate judgment of mankind, and the gracious favor of Almighty God.

In testimony whereof, I have hereunto set my name, and caused the seal of the United States to be affixed.

Done at the City of Washington, this first day of January, in the year of our Lord one thousand eight hundred and sixty-three, and of the independence of the United States the eighty-seventh.

By the President,
ABRAHAM LINCOLN

WILLIAM H. SEWARD,
Secretary of State.

91. Effects of the Proclamation. It is to be observed that the Proclamation was merely a war measure resting on the constitutional power of the President. Its effects on the legal status of the slaves gave rise to much discussion; and one may note that it did not apply to what is now West Virginia, to seven counties in Virginia, and to thirteen parishes in Louisiana, which districts had already come under federal jurisdiction. All questions raised by the measure, however, were finally settled by the Thirteenth Amendment to the Constitution, and freedom actually followed the progress of the American arms from 1863 to 1865. The moral effect of the Proclamation was such as Lincoln had foreseen, and the more radical elements in the North now rallied to his support.

92. Conflicting Policies as to Negro Troops. Negroes were used by the Confederates long before they saw service with the Union forces. Even before the war began the slaves were employed in making redoubts and in other rough work. Before the war was over, when the South was hard pressed, plans for the formation of Negro regiments in the Confederate armies were seriously proposed, and General Robert E. Lee was one of those who advocated such a policy. All such effort was, of course, at variance with the main tendencies of the period in the seceded slaveholding states.

The Negro is naturally remembered most quickly in connection with the Union armies. In May, 1861, while in command at Fortress Monroe, Major-General Benjamin F. Butler gained prominence by receiving fugitive slaves within his lines. These men he put to work, justifying their retention on the ground that, being of service to the enemy, they were, like guns and powder, contraband of war and could not be reclaimed. On August 30 of this same year Major-General John C. Frémont, in command in Missouri, placed the state under martial law and declared the slaves there emancipated. The administration was embarrassed, Frémont's order was annulled, and he was relieved of his command. On May 9, 1862, Major-General David Hunter, in charge of the Department of the South (that is, South Carolina, Georgia, and Florida), issued an order freeing the slaves in his department, and thus brought to general attention the matter of the employment of Negro soldiers in the Union armies. The Confederate government outlawed Hunter, Lincoln annulled his order, and the grace of the nation was again saved; but in the meantime a new situation arose. While Brigadier-General John W. Phelps was taking part in the expedition against New Orleans, a large sugar planter near the city, disgusted with Federal interference with affairs on his plantation, drove all the slaves away, telling them to go to their friends, the Yankees. The Negroes came to Phelps in great numbers, and he attempted to organize them into troops. Accordingly he too was outlawed by the Confederates, and his act was disavowed by the Union, which was not as yet ready to take the step of enlisting the Negro.

It was not until a great many men had been killed, and until the Emancipation Proclamation had changed the status of the Negro, that steps were formally taken by the Union for his employment as a soldier. The leading spirit in advocating such employment was John A. Andrew, the great-hearted governor of Massachusetts, who had the idea of a "sample regiment" of such high quality as to lead to the formation of others. In Washington he conferred at length with Edwin M. Stanton, Secretary of War, and at last persuaded him as to the advisability of the plan. Thus it was that on January 26, 1863, Governor Andrew received from the Secretary of War an order to raise such number of volunteer companies as he might find convenient, the volunteers to enlist for three years, or until sooner discharged, and to "include persons of African descent, organized into separate corps." This was the beginning of the famous Fifty-Fourth Massachusetts Regiment. By the close of the war a little more than 186,000 Negroes had been enrolled in the Union armies.

93. The Negro in the Civil War. The Negro troops were particularly distinguished for their heroism at Port Hudson, Fort Wagner, Fort Pillow, and around Petersburg.

Some important operations culminated on July 8, 1863, in the capture of the Confederate batteries at Port Hudson, a small village on the left bank of the Mississippi River, about 135 miles above New Orleans. A Negro regiment was prominent in the operations of the siege on May 27th, and worked with such valor that a correspondent of the *New York Times* said of the men, "Their colors are torn to pieces by shot, and literally bespattered by blood and brains." This was the occasion on which Color-Sergeant Anselmas Planciançois said before a shell blew off his head, "Colonel, I will bring back these colors to you on honor, or report to God the reason why." On June 6th the Negroes again distinguished themselves and won friends by their bravery at Milliken's Bend.

The Fifty-Fourth Massachusetts, commanded by Colonel Robert Gould Shaw, was conspicuous in the attempt to take Fort Wagner, on Morris Island near Charleston, July 18, 1863. The regiment had marched two days and two nights through swamps and drenching rains in order to be in time for the assault. In the engagement nearly all the officers of the regiment were killed, among them Colonel Shaw. The picturesque deed was that of Sergeant William H. Carney, who seized the regiment's colors from the hand of a falling comrade and planted the flag on the works, saying when borne bleeding and mangled from the scene, "Boys, the old flag never touched the ground."

Fort Pillow, a position on the Mississippi about fifty miles above Memphis, was when attacked April 13, 1864, garrisoned by 557 men, 262 of whom were Negroes. The fort was taken by the Confederates, but the feature of the engagement was the stubborn resistance offered by the Union troops in the face of great odds.

In the spring of 1864 Negro troops were in the Army of the Potomac in the operations around Richmond and

Petersburg, and in July figured in a gallant charge on the Confederates in this vital region.

94. Northern Leaders. Of the commanders of Negro troops there were some who call for special notice.

Robert Gould Shaw, a young Harvard man in the Union army, representative of the fine flower of New England manhood, was offered the colonelcy of the Fifty-Fourth Massachusetts, the first regiment of Negro troops raised in a Northern state. He accepted. After taking part in an expedition to the Southern coast, he led his men in the attack on Fort Wagner and was himself killed upon the parapet of the fort. A monument to him and to his regiment designed by Augustus St. Gaudens stands now at the head of Boston Common just in front of the Massachusetts State House.

Another distinguished commander of Negro troops was Thomas Wentworth Higginson, who became colonel of the first regiment of freed slaves raised in the United States. By reason of a wound received in a campaign in Florida in 1863 Colonel Higginson was forced to retire from the service, and after the war he devoted himself to literature and public affairs.

Also outstanding for their faith and heroism were Norwood Penrose Hallowell, lieutenant-colonel of the Fifty-Fourth and later colonel of the Fifty-Fifth, and his brother, Edward N. Hallowell, who succeeded Shaw when he fell.

CHAPTER IX

ENFRANCHISEMENT

95. Difficulties of the Situation.   On arriving at the era of Reconstruction, we come to that period which is still the most warmly debated in American history. The difficulties of the situation are even yet not fully ap-- preciated.

The Civil War meant more than the emancipation of four million slaves; it involved the overturning of the whole economic system of the South. A stroke of the pen had declared the bondmen free; but to educate these people, to train them in citizenship, and to give them a place in the new labor system, was all a problem for the wisest statesmanship and the most intelligent patriotism. The Southern man, whose fortune was swept away, whose slaves were free, and whose father, son, or brother had died in battle, not unnaturally looked upon any legislation by the North as but adding to his humiliation. The North on the other hand was quick to interpret any effort by the white South in the readjustment of social and labor conditions as evidence of a refusal to accept in good faith the results of the war.

To increase the complication there were sometimes present personal or other elements that seemed to contradict all the leading tendencies of the period. Some Negroes, for instance, personally attached to their masters, were not eager to accept their freedom; and throughout the South the white people, who laid most of their ills at the door of the Negro, resisted any considerable effort toward migration on the part of the former slaves. Such were but some of the difficulties to be met in solving the problems of this era of shifting status.

96. Theories of Reconstruction.   According to the view of their status maintained by the Southern states at the close of the war, each state was theoretically indestructible, and the only thing necessary for one to resume its former place in the nation was for it, having laid down its arms, to repeal all acts that looked toward disunion.

In the view of President Lincoln, the act of rebellion had been one not of the states themselves but of certain disloyal persons who had subverted the government. Each *state* then continued to exist, and the problem presented was simply to place the loyal elements in control. As this involved the use of the pardoning power, the President regarded the matter as one for executive rather than legislative authority.

Opposed to this was the opinion of Congress embodied in the Wade-Davis act of 1864, differing from the President's view in regarding the problem primarily as a legislative one, in requiring the loyalty of a majority of the white voters of a state as the basis of a reconstructed government instead of that of the one tenth of the qualified voters of 1860 advocated by Lincoln, and in exacting for the Negro the full reality of his freedom. The leaders of this school of opinion were Charles Sumner, of Massachusetts, in the Senate, and Thaddeus Stevens, of Pennsylvania, in the House of Representatives.

The breach which opened between the President and Congress because of these conflicting views might have closed by Lincoln's tact, but on his death the solution of the problem fell to the lot of a less able statesman. It was President Johnson, who, on May 29, 1865, issued a proclamation of amnesty with the understanding attached that those excluded from its benefits might make special application to him, and who, within the next few months, while Congress was not in session, worked out generally Lincoln's theory of reconstruction. In December the President informed Congress that, with the exception of Texas whose convention did not meet until the following March, all the states had been reconstructed and were ready to resume their places in Congress. Because, however, of certain legislation in Mississippi, South Carolina, and Louisiana, embodied in what were known as the Black Codes, Congress doubted whether the states were acting in good faith. The Black Codes were in the nature of police regulations designed to prevent disorder and pauperism among the freedmen, but they led to the thought that they were designed to curtail for the former slaves the benefits of emancipation; and there was probability that other states would go quite as far as those mentioned.

97. The War Amendments. In the meantime the Thirteenth Amendment to the Constitution had been sufficiently ratified and was passed (December 18, 1865). It read as follows: "Neither slavery nor involuntary servitude, except as a punishment for crime whereof the party shall have been duly convicted, shall exist within the United States, or any place subject to their jurisdiction. Congress shall have power to enforce this article by appropriate legislation."

In March, 1866, Congress passed over the President's veto the first Civil Rights Bill, guaranteeing to the freedmen all the ordinary rights of citizenship; and it enlarged the powers of the Freedmen's Bureau, which had recently been established. At this point feeling in the North was intensified by some violent attacks on Negroes and white radicals in the South, especially by one such affair in New Orleans in which about forty men were killed and one hundred and fifty wounded. When Congress met in December, 1866, it endeavored to impeach President Johnson. Failing in this, by various measures it limited his power, established Negro suffrage in the District of Columbia and in the territories, and passed two more war amendments to reinforce its own reconstruction program.

The Fourteenth Amendment, as finally passed by Congress (July 28, 1868), denied to the states the power to abridge the privileges or immunities of citizens of the United States, or to deprive any person of life, liberty, or property without due process of law; and enacted that if a state discriminated against any class of citizens in voting privileges, its representation in the national Congress was to be reduced proportionately.

The Fifteenth Amendment (passed March 30, 1870) read: "The right of citizens of the United States to vote shall not be denied or abridged by the United States or by any state, on account of race, color, or previous condition of servitude. The Congress shall have power to enforce this article by appropriate legislation."

98. The Freedmen's Bureau. Even before the close of the war the Government had been forced to formulate a policy with reference to the thousands of Negroes who crowded to the Federal lines. By an act of March 3, 1865, there was created the Bureau of Refugee Freedmen and Abandoned Lands, commonly known as the Freedmen's Bureau. This agency was to have control of all matters relating to refugees and freedmen. Of special importance in the creating act was a provision that gave the freedmen to understand that each male refugee would be given forty acres with a guarantee of possession for three years, a promise that was never fulfilled.

This agency was to remain in existence throughout the war and for one year thereafter, but its powers were continued and enlarged by an act of July 16, 1866. While the chief work of the Bureau was completed by January 1, 1869, its educational interests continued for a year and a half longer.

Throughout the existence of the Bureau its chief commissioner was General Oliver Otis Howard, who in connection with his activities became the first president of Howard University. Other prominent officials were similarly men of noble purpose, but many of the minor officials were corrupt and self-seeking. Thus it happened that the Bureau did not accomplish all that it was hoped it might. Moreover, morally though not technically connected with it was the Freedmen's Savings and Trust Company, commonly known as the

Freedmen's Bank, which made a remarkable start in thrift on the part of the Negroes, and the failure of which had the most disastrous consequences.[1]

99. Reconstruction Governments. After Congress failed in its attempt to impeach President Johnson, and when it saw that the Southern states were disposed to reject the proposed Fourteenth Amendment, it proceeded to divide the ten states which had seceded into five military districts, as follows: (1) Virginia, (2) North and South Carolina, (3) Georgia, Florida, and Alabama, (4) Mississippi and Arkansas, (5) Louisiana and Texas. Military law thus protected everybody in the enjoyment of his rights, and federal authorities oversaw the registering and voting of all men without regard to race or color.

By February, 1868, constitutional conventions were in session in every state that had seceded. These were made up mainly of the Negro freedmen, of Northern white men who had come South since the war and were called in derision "carpetbaggers," and of Southern white men who acted at variance with the dominant sentiment of the South and were known as "scalawags." After the passing of the Fifteenth Amendment "carpetbag" governments set up by these conventions were in full career, and there set in an era of extravagance and increasing debt in which for the most part not the Negro himself but those who exploited him reaped the benefit. Secret organizations, of which the Union League was the best

[1] For a readable account of the Freedmen's Bureau, not too long, see W. E. B. DuBois, *The Souls of Black Folk* (Chicago: A. C McCherg & Co., 1903), Chapter II.

example, were formed for marshalling the Negro vote in the South for the Republican party.

It is the events of this period that the so-called "unreconstructed South" has never ceased to lament. Year after year publicists, historians, and novelists have upbraided Congress for the acts that enfranchised the former slaves and protected them in the enjoyment of their rights. Especially have they besmirched the memory of Charles Sumner and Thaddeus Stevens, and left documents favorable to the Negro out of court. That the picture was overdrawn, that many of the Negroes who came into prominence were men of intelligence and character, that some of the acts of the Reconstruction governments, such as those affecting public education, marked great advance, has been shown by Dr. W. E. B. DuBois in his notable work, *Black Reconstruction.*

However, it was not long after the war before the white South determined not to accept the new order, and then the Ku Klux Klan began its operations. The race issue was the dominant one in the presidential election of 1876, and in South Carolina there was a notable overturn, with the invasion of Negro homes and the slaughter of more than thirty persons in massacres at Hamburg and Ellenton. Soon the withdrawal of Federal troops and the removal by Congress of disabilities on former Confederates weakened the Reconstruction governments, and the Democrats again became supreme in the South.

100. The Negro in Congress. Deserving of notice in this interesting period is the large number of Negroes that Reconstruction brought into prominence.

The freedmen were not only active in Southern

legislatures, but were also sometimes sent to Congress. The first Negro to serve as United States senator, and the first man of the race to appear in either house of Congress, was Hiram R. Revels, of Mississippi, who completed an unexpired term and actually served from February 25, 1870, to March 3, 1871. The second senator, and the first to serve a full term, was Blanche K. Bruce, of Mississippi, who was in office from March 4, 1875, to March 3, 1881. In the House of Representatives fourteen Negroes were seated before 1876. The first to appear, and the one who was in office longer than any other, was Joseph H. Rainey, of South Carolina, who actually served from December 12, 1870, until March 3, 1879. South Carolina was also represented by Robert C. DeLarge, Robert B. Elliott, Richard H. Cain, Alonzo J. Ransier, and Robert Smalls; Alabama by Benjamin S. Turner, James T. Rapier, and Jeremiah Haralson; Mississippi by John R. Lynch, Georgia by Jefferson Long, Florida by Josiah T. Walls, North Carolina by John A. Hyman, and Louisiana by Charles E. Nash.

P. B. S. Pinchback served as lieutenant-governor and then as acting governor in Louisiana; Oscar J. Dunn and C. C. Antoine were for three and four years respectively lieutenant-governors in the same state; Alonzo J. Ransier and Richard H. Gleaves held this position in South Carolina; and Alexander K. Davis in Mississippi.

Of all these men the foremost for general ability were Robert B. Elliott and Blanche K. Bruce. Elliott was born in Jamaica, but was taken by his parents while still young to Boston, Massachusetts. He received good early training in England, and, returning to America, studied law and developed highly the arts of a politician. In Congress he attracted attention by a brilliant speech in reply to Alexander Stephens and other Southern men on the constitutionality of the second Civil Rights Bill. Bruce was well informed on matters pertaining to his race; he also took a broad view of public affairs; and in the course of his life he held several public offices besides the senatorship. For two terms (1881-1885 and 1897-1898) he was Register of the Treasury.

101. The Ku Klux Klan.   Worthy also of note in this era of change is the means by which the white people of the South regained political power. Even before the war a secret organization, the Knights of the Golden Circle, had been formed to advance Southern interests; but far more important than anything of this nature that had preceded it was the Ku Klux Klan.[2] This organization began in Tennessee in 1866 as an association of young men for amusement, but it soon developed into a union for the whipping, banishing, terrorizing, and murdering of the Negroes and of the Northern white men who worked with them. The costume of the members was designed to play upon the superstitious nature of the uneducated Negroes. Most often it was a long white garment, with loose, flowing sleeves, a hood with horns, and openings for the mouth and eyes trimmed with some red material. The Ku Klux Klan finally extended over the whole South, and it greatly increased its operations on the cessation of martial law in 1870. As it worked generally at night with its members in disguise, it was difficult for a grand jury to get evidence

[2] From the Greek κύκλος meaning *circle*, and the English *clan*.

on which to frame a bill, and almost impossible to secure a conviction. Repeated measures against the order were of little effect until an act extended the jurisdiction of the United States courts to all Ku Klux cases; then gradually the order declined.

102. The Negro Exodus. The aftermath of the whole Reconstruction era was what was known as the Negro Exodus. By 1879 conditions in the South had changed so much that Negroes were denied political recognition, charged excessive rents, forced into practical peonage, and generally kept down in every way. At last in some localities, especially in South Carolina, Mississippi, Louisiana, and Texas, the state of affairs became so bad as to be no longer tolerable.

A convention of Negroes held in Nashville in May, 1879, adopted a report that set forth their grievances and encouraged emigration to the North and West, where rights would not be denied. Thousands of Negroes then left their homes in the South, going in greatest numbers to Kansas, Missouri, and Indiana. Within twenty months Kansas alone thus received an addition to her population of 40,000 Negroes. Many of these people arrived at their destination almost penniless and without prospect of immediate employment; but large sums of money for their relief were raised in the North, and gradually they found a place in their new homes.

In the Southeast there was also effort in another direction. In 1877 the Liberian Exodus Joint Stock Company was formed by Negroes for the threefold purpose of sending emigrants to Africa, of bringing

African products to America, and of establishing a regular steamship line between Monrovia and Charleston. In this enterprise Baptists and Methodists joined hands, and at an expense of $7,000 a vessel, the *Azor*, was purchased in Boston. The white people of Charleston, who did not wish to lose their domestic help, embarrassed the promoters by every means possible. Although the *Azor* had recently been repaired in Boston, they induced the custom house officials not to grant it clearance papers until a new copper bottom had been put on it at a cost of $2,000. Then not all the people the vessel would hold were allowed to go on the first trip. Finally, through the connivance of the captain with some business men in Charleston, the *Azor* was stolen and sold in Liverpool. One sees an interesting sidelight on conditions in these times when he knows that even the United States Circuit Court in South Carolina refused to entertain the suit brought by the Negroes.

BOOKER T. WASHINGTON, GREAT NEGRO EDUCATOR

CHAPTER X

EFFORT IN EDUCATION

103. Periods. In 1860 not less than nine out of every ten Negroes in the country were illiterate, and even before the Civil War was over it was realized that the freedmen should have training for citizenship. We have observed the interest of the Reconstruction governments of the South in public education; higher training for more than a generation was promoted chiefly by missionary agencies in the North.

In Negro education in general since the Civil War one might note several periods. First, from 1865 to 1876, there was the period of temporary army and mission schools, though even in these years were laid the foundations of some institutions that became colleges. Next came a decade of effort toward the building of complete school systems, with normal schools and colleges training teachers for the public schools. Then for three decades there was emphasis on industrial training. This was given impetus by the establishment of the John F. Slater Fund in 1882, and gained wide acceptance after the speech of Booker T. Washington at the Atlanta Exposition in 1895. In 1908, with the founding of the Jeanes Fund, there began a notable development of rural schools. After the World War came a new recognition of the value of collegiate training, with emphasis on the expansion of the so-called land-grant colleges. Finally, since 1930, there has been effort toward the consolidation of the work in various groups of colleges and in different geographical centers.

104. The Pioneers. Too much credit can hardly be given to the heroic men and women who labored in the early years. Those people of the North who took upon themselves the education of the Negro immediately after the war had no enviable task. They had as their portion prejudice and ostracism, and an infinite amount of hard work; and their only reward was a sense of duty well done.

Where so many were noble it is almost unjust to mention names; but in any case deserving of honor were General Samuel C. Armstrong at Hampton, President E. M. Cravath at Fisk, President Henry M. Tupper at Shaw, President Asa Ware at the old Atlanta University, and, of a slightly later date, at Spelman College, Presidents Sophia B. Packard and Harriet E. Giles. Just as earnest as such teachers as these were those who devoted themselves to mission work in the homes of the freemen, of whom a sterling example was Joanna P. Moore, who labored for fifty years in the cause of her Fireside Schools.

105. Philanthropy. For the execution of the task at hand money was needed, and private philanthropy was not lacking, though even the most princely gifts were inadequate for the work to be done.

In 1867 George Peabody, a great American merchant and patriot, established the Peabody Education Fund "for the promotion and encouragement of intellectual, moral, or industrial education among the young of the more destitute portions of the Southern and South-western states of our Union." An original gift of $1,000,000 was later increased to $2,384,000, and it was provided that the benefits should be distributed among the entire population "without other distinctions than their needs and the opportunities of usefulness to them." The trustees co-operated with state and local authorities, and both races in the South were helped by this great contribution to public education.

When the Peabody foundation was dissolved in 1914, the sum of $350,000 remaining on hand was given to the John F. Slater Fund, which was specifically for the Negro. This latter foundation was established by a manufacturer of Norwich, Connecticut, who in 1882 set aside $1,000,000 for "the uplifting of the lately emancipated population of the Southern states, and their posterity, by conferring on them the blessings of Chris-tian education."

Six years later Daniel Hand, also of Connecticut, gave $1,000,000 to the American Missionary Associa-tion for its educational work in the South. The General Education Board, the medium of the philanthropy of John D. Rockefeller, was organized in 1902. It has shown interest in all phases of Negro education and up to 1930 had made contributions amounting to not less than $22,000,000.

In November, 1907, was incorporated the Negro Rural School Fund, Anna T. Jeanes Foundation, com-monly known as the Jeanes Fund, "for the purpose of assisting in the Southern United States community, country, and rural schools for the great class of Negroes to whom the small rural and community schools are alone available." Anna T. Jeanes was a Quaker of Philadelphia whose interest in rural schools had been awakened by Hollis B. Frissell, then principal of Hampton Institute, and by Booker T. Washington. She had made previous contributions, but her permanent foundation was established by a special gift of $1,000,000. Dr. J. H. Dillard, formerly professor and dean at Tulane University, became director of the trust, and two years later he began his connection also with the Slater Fund, of which in 1917 he formally became president. He thus in course of time directed from one office the Jeanes Fund, the Slater Fund, and what was left of the Peabody Fund. In 1931, when Dr. Dillard was succeeded by Dr. Arthur D. Wright, the co-operating agencies were formally united as the Southern Education Foundation.

In 1914 the Julius Rosenwald Fund began its work, its special contribution being the erecting of rural school buildings with the co-operation of county school boards and the Negro people themselves. The first efforts were modest, but by 1930 the fund had assisted in the building of more than five thousand schools, with an expenditure of not less than $4,000,000. Mr. Rosenwald also gave valiant help in the erecting of Y. M. C. A. buildings for Negro men and boys.

Other notable benefactions within recent years have included, in Delaware, the Pierre S. Du Pont gift, by which every Negro school district in the state was assured a modern building on a minimum site of two acres, and, in North Carolina, the Duke Foundation, special beneficiaries of which are Johnson C. Smith University and Kittrell College. The Phelps-Stokes Fund and the Carnegie Corporation of New York have also assisted from time to time in special phases of educational endeavor.

106. **Howard University.** In addition to such private giving as this, the United States Government in 1867 crowned its educational work for the Negro with the founding in Washington of Howard University. This institution, named for General O. O. Howard, has stood for the highest collegiate and professional training. Its College of Medicine is widely known; within recent years there has been a notable development of the Graduate School; and to the resources of its own laboratories and libraries the University adds the advantages of an institution located at the national capital and fostered by the Government. In 1926 it called to the helm its first president of Negro descent, Dr. Mordecai W. Johnson; and within twelve years after he took office, aside from internal improvements, the institution had been almost completely rebuilt. There were erected three new dormitories for women, two for men, a power plant, a large Chemistry Building, a recitation building named Frederick Douglass Memorial Hall, and, greatest of all, The Founders Library. In 1938 Howard enrolled in all schools and departments 2,240 students, 1,360 being in the College of Liberal Arts.

107. **The American Missionary Association.** In the far South the chief efforts in higher education were those put forth by the various missionary agencies of the

North. One of the unfortunate features of missionary endeavor was the utter independence of the work of the different religious organizations. In some centers there was a duplication of effort, and naturally there has been within recent years a demand for reorganization and consolidation.

The American Missionary Association was the first of all the benevolent agencies to begin work. It was organized before the Civil War on an interdenominational and strong antislavery basis, but in 1881 passed into the control of the Congregational Church. It opened its first school in Hampton, Virginia, in 1881, and immediately after the war founded its permanent institutions. The plan was to establish one college in each of the larger states of the South, normal and graded schools in the principal cities, and common or parochial schools in smaller villages and country places. Obviously this attempted too much, and in course of time, as the Southern states improved their public-school facilities, the Association tended to withdraw not only from the elementary- but also from the secondary-school work.

Under the original plan, however, arose Hampton in Virginia, Atlanta University in Georgia, Berea College in Kentucky, Fisk University in Tennessee, Straight University in Louisiana, Talladega College in Alabama, Tougaloo University in Mississippi, and Tillotson College in Texas. Hampton and Fisk are now independent, and Berea has had a peculiar history, legislation early in the century having compelled the withdrawal of its Negro students. Fisk has an excellent library, has maintained high scholastic standards, and is well known for its emphasis on music. One of the most inspiring chapters in its history is the record of the Fisk Jubilee Singers. As the result of consolidation within recent years, the work of Talladega has been greatly enhanced; Atlanta University, removed from its old location and reorganized as an independent institution, has become the head of a new university system in Atlanta; and Straight has helped to form a new center of higher training, Dillard University. LeMoyne College, Memphis, Tennessee, which was long simply a secondary school, has now been raised to college rank. The American Missionary Association has emphasized manual and industrial as well as collegiate training, and Talladega was one of the first of all Negro institutions to establish an industrial department.

108. The American Baptist Home Mission Society. The first step by the American Baptist Home Mission Society in behalf of the refugees who came within the Union lines, was taken in January, 1862; and the first teachers were appointed in June of that year. The Society emphasized religious education; and the idea of a well-trained ministry becomes important when one remembers how great an influence preachers have with the Negro people, and how numerous are the Baptists. The work of the Society expanded until it embraced a chain of educational institutions, and much assistance was also given to schools owned and operated by Negro Baptist organizations.

There have been many changes, but about 1925 the institutions that the Society operated (sometimes in cooperation with the Woman's American Baptist Home

Mission Society) were nine in number, as follows: one devoted solely to the education of young men, More-house College in Atlanta, Georgia; one devoted to the training of young women, Spelman College in Atlanta, Georgia; and seven that were coeducational—Virginia Union University in Richmond, Virginia; Shaw Uni-versity in Raleigh, North Carolina; Benedict College in Columbia, South Carolina; Storer College at Harpers Ferry, West Virginia; Jackson College in Jackson, Mississippi; Leland College at Baker, Louisiana; and Bishop College at Marshall, Texas.

Since 1925, however, Spelman (named for the family of the wife of John D. Rockefeller) has greatly out-stripped the other institutions in endowment; More-house, Shaw, and Virginia Union have become increas-ingly if not quite independent; both Spelman and More-house have been drawn into the university system now developing in Atlanta; and in general the educational work of the American Baptist Home Mission Society has been taken over by the Board of Education of the Northern Baptist Convention. Shaw was the first Negro college in the progressive state of North Carolina to be recognized as of "A" grade and the first south of Washington to do away with all high-school work. Virginia Union has made rapid advance within recent years, receiving notable increase to its endowment, and Morehouse has been outstanding for its emphasis on all phases of manly endeavor. Spelman is the foremost college in the world devoted solely to the education of young Negro women. The plant is unusually impressive, the Sisters Chapel being of unique distinction; and in the record of graduates who have gone as missionaries to Africa, this institution has a tradition as glorious as that of the Fisk Jubilee Singers.

In connection with the American Baptist Home Mission Society mention must also be made of the American Baptist Publication Society. For some years after the Civil War this organization worked for the education of Negro Baptist ministers and the upbuilding of churches and Sunday schools, distributing large quantities of literature, but its activities were later somewhat curtailed by the advance of distinctively Negro publishing houses.

109. The Freedmen's Aid Society.   As will be seen later, consideration of the educational work of most of the Methodist denominations belongs to the story of self-help in Negro education; but the Methodist Episcopal Church (that is, the main body of northern Methodists) organized in 1866 the Freedmen's Aid Society, which was distinctly missionary in purpose. In 1882, by act of the General Conference, the Board of Managers was instructed to aid schools for needy white people in the South as far as it could do so without embarrassing its work for the Negroes, and the name of the governing organization became the Freedmen's Aid and Southern Education Society.[1] In 1908 the General Conference reversed the action of 1882, effort for the two races was separated, and that for the Negro was again conducted by the Freedmen's Aid Society. In 1920 the name

[1] For a full review of the work of the Freedmen's Aid Society, see D. O. W. Holmes, *The Evolution of the Negro College* (New York: Bureau of Publications, Teachers College, Columbia University, 1934), pp. 102-119.

of the Society was changed to "Board of Education for Negroes of the Methodist Episcopal Church," and four years later this was merged with the general Board of Education of the Methodist Episcopal Church.

These changes in the name of the Society are representative of the changes that have taken place in the institutions it operated. In course of time there were not less than twenty of these, and ten were collegiate in scope. The list of those that have been best known at one time or another would include Bennett College for Women, Greensboro, North Carolina; Claflin University, Orangeburg, South Carolina; Clark University, Atlanta, Georgia; Central Tennessee College, later Walden, Nashville, Tennessee; Bethune-Cookman College, Daytona Beach, Florida; New Orleans University, New Orleans, Louisiana; Rust College, Holly Springs, Mississippi; Philander Smith College, Little Rock, Arkansas; Samuel Huston College, Austin, Texas; and Wiley University, Marshall, Texas. A theological school in Baltimore developed into what is now Morgan College; and there have also been two medical schools, Meharry Medical College, Nashville, Tennessee, and the New Orleans Medical College, New Orleans, Louisiana.

Central Tennessee College, Clark, and Claflin were among the earlier institutions to emphasize industrial training. Courses in tailoring, plumbing, iron and wood working, harness making, painting, printing, and other trades were provided for the young men, and there were also special courses for the young women. Central Tennessee (Walden) was closed about the time of the World War; but the Meharry Medical College, with which it was in close affiliation, has developed into a strong institution by reason of a $550,000 endowment created in 1921. New Orleans University was merged in the present Dillard University; and the New Orleans Medical College survives only as the Flint Goodrich Hospital, affiliated with Dillard. Morgan has come more and more under the patronage of the state of Maryland, and Clark has been removed from its old site in South Atlanta and in 1938 was being rebuilt as a unit in the new Atlanta University system.

Meanwhile Bennett College for Women, by reason of an alert policy and special gifts, and Bethune-Cookman (the union of an independent institution founded by Mary McLeod Bethune, and Cookman Institute, formerly in Jacksonville) have steadily advanced, and Wiley has become more and more outstanding in the Southwest.

Gammon Theological Seminary, in South Atlanta, Ga., was also founded under the auspices of the Methodist Episcopal Church. As an institution for the special training of Negro ministers, it is the best endowed and the most thoroughly equipped in the world.

110. **The Presbyterian Board of Missions.** The Presbyterians began educational work for the Negro in the South as early as 1865, but in 1883 the central committee directing their activities became incorporated as "The Board of Missions for Freedmen of the Presbyterian Church in the United States of America." This organization has been active in both school and college work; as early as 1871 not less than forty-five parochial

or other schools were being conducted under Presbyterian auspices for the education of the Negro.

Even before the Civil War, in 1854, a minister of the denomination, John M. Dickey, established Ashmun Institute in Pennsylvania. In 1866 the institution thus founded received a charter under the name of Lincoln University. Lincoln now has an independent board of trustees, but its theological school is controlled by the Presbyterians, and in general it is in close touch with that group of Christians.

The larger part of the work of the Board lies in North Carolina, South Carolina, and southern Virginia. Its foremost institution in these states is Johnson C. Smith University, in Charlotte, N. C. This college, formerly known as Biddle University, received its present name in 1923 after Mrs. Johnson C. Smith, of Pittsburgh, Pennsylvania, began contributions which ultimately amounted to more than $700,000. From an endowment trust set up by the will of the late James B. Duke, the institution will also receive a sum approaching $1,500,000. In 1932 there became affiliated with Johnson C. Smith the Barber-Scotia College, of Concord, North Carolina, which represented the merging and development of two of the seminaries for young women conducted by the Board.

Considerable educational work is also being done by the United and the Southern Presbyterians, the United Presbyterians maintaining Knoxville College, in Knoxville, Tennessee.

111. Other Religious Agencies. The four large denominations just considered bore for more than a generation the brunt of the responsibility for the high-school and collegiate training of the Negro. The institutions under state auspices were not yet fully developed. The Congregationalists, the Baptists, the Methodists, and the Presbyterians, however, are not the only religious groups that have shown interest in the work.

The Quakers and Unitarians have made steady contributions, in large or small amounts, most often to institutions of which they were not in charge.

The American Church Institute for Negroes, the agency of the Protestant Episcopal Church, has maintained St. Augustine's College, Raleigh, North Carolina, and three secondary schools that have developed into junior colleges—the St. Paul Normal and Industrial Institute, Lawrenceville, Virginia, the Fort Valley Normal and Industrial Institute, Fort Valley, Georgia, and St. Philip's Junior College, San Antonio, Texas.

The Roman Catholics have conducted more than a hundred elementary or secondary schools; but up to 1938 their one institution of full college grade was Xavier University, New Orleans, Louisiana. In 1929 a new site for this college was secured, and two years later the construction of three buildings was begun. These include a faculty building, a science hall, and a large central building for administration and school work. As there are many Catholics in the vicinity of New Orleans, Xavier has naturally made rapid advance within recent years.

112. Land-Grant Colleges. When we turn from colleges maintained by religious agencies to those operated under state or governmental auspices, we immediately face a group of institutions that calls for special consideration, as in the case of the land-grant colleges.

The so-called land-grant colleges go back in their history to a bill first presented in Congress by Senator Justin S. Morrill, of Vermont, and passed in 1862. This provided "that there be granted to the several states an amount of public land, to be apportioned to each state a quantity equal to 30,000 acres for each Senator and Representative in Congress to which the states are respectively entitled by the apportionment under the census of 1860," the proceeds to go to institutions emphasizing agriculture and mechanic arts. The provisions of the act were not carried out without discrimination against the Negro until the second Morrill Act (1890) forbade payment of any appropriation to any college that made in admitting students a distinction based on race or color. As a student of the subject says, the act was "unique in that the national government set up separate schools for white and colored students, thereby retreating from the finer hopes of democratic government." [2]

There were seventeen institutions designated in the different states as land-grant colleges, as follows: State Agricultural and Mechanical College, Normal, Alabama; Agricultural, Mechanical and Normal College, Pine Bluff, Arkansas; State College for Colored Students, Dover, Delaware; Florida Agricultural and Mechanical College, Tallahassee, Florida; Georgia State Industrial

[2] John W. Davis, *Land-Grant Colleges for Negroes,* Publications of West Virginia State College (Institute, West Virginia, 1915), p. 13.

College, Industrial College, Georgia; Kentucky State Industrial College, Frankfort, Kentucky; Southern University and Agricultural and Mechanical College, Baton Rouge, Louisiana; Princess Anne College, Princess Anne, Maryland; Alcorn Agricultural and Mechanical College, Alcorn, Mississippi; Lincoln University, Jefferson City, Missouri; Negro Agricultural and Technical College, Greensboro, North Carolina; Colored Agricultural and Normal University, Langston, Oklahoma; Colored Normal, Agricultural and Mechanical College, Orangeburg, South Carolina; Agricultural and Industrial State Normal College for Negroes, Nashville, Tennessee; Prairie View State Normal and Industrial College, Prairie View, Texas; Virginia State College for Negroes, Petersburg, Virginia; and West Virginia State College, Institute, West Virginia.

The result of the establishing of separate institutions was soon seen. The military training emphasized in the organizing act is seldom given in the Negro colleges, and in 1934 it was observed: "Unlike many of the land-grant institutions for white students, not one of the Land-Grant Colleges for Negroes offers any professional or graduate work. Moreover, not one of the 17 states in which there are separate land-grant institutions for Negroes has made a worth-while effort to provide professional training for Negroes within the state." [3] Since 1934 some test cases have forced different states to face the situation, but the main point still holds.

Yet, with all of the disadvantages, the advance of

[3] Ibid., 43.

this group of colleges within the last two decades has been remarkable, and in some instances (notably Virginia State, Tennessee State, and Prairie View) highly exceptional. Interest has been shown by the General Education Board and the Rosenwald Fund, and this has helped to cultivate a more liberal attitude, especially in Virginia, Alabama, Oklahoma, and Tennessee.

113. Other State or City Institutions. It must not be supposed that the land-grant colleges are the only state or city institutions for higher training. In some instances this is so, and a single school undertakes to offer collegiate, normal, and agricultural courses; but sometimes there is also in the state a normal school, or even a liberal arts college. In North Carolina, aside from the Agricultural and Technical College in Greensboro, one finds in Durham the North Carolina College for Negroes, in Winston-Salem the Winston-Salem Teachers College, also two-year normal schools in Elizabeth City and Fayetteville. In West Virginia there is at Bluefield the Bluefield State Teachers College; in Alabama, at Montgomery, is the large Alabama State Teachers College; and in Maryland one finds, in Baltimore, the Fannie Jackson Coppin Normal School, and at Bowie the Maryland State Normal School. In Washington, D. C., is the well-appointed Miner Teachers College; in Cheyney, Pennsylvania, is the Cheyney Training School for Teachers, one of the state colleges for teachers; and in Louisville, Kentucky, a new and interesting line of development is suggested by the Municipal College for Negroes.

114. Self-Help in the Public Schools. To what extent, in all of this development, was the Negro himself a directly contributing factor?

As early as 1869 General Howard reported that the recently emancipated freedmen had in one year raised for the construction of schoolhouses and the support of teachers not less than $200,000.

Since 1870 common-school education has been conducted chiefly by the states, and Negro contributions have been mainly through taxes, though not exclusively so. While there is no source from which accurate conclusions may be drawn, it seems likely that the Negroes have paid for the entire amount of public-school training which they have received from the Southern states since 1870. This does not mean that the direct taxes on the property of the Negroes have been sufficient to pay for their common-school education, for they have not; but neither have the direct taxes on the property of the white people been sufficient to pay for their common-school education. In Georgia, when everything is considered, it becomes evident that the Negroes are in no sense a burden on the white taxpayers, and that, although they pay hundreds of thousands of dollars each year to white people for rent, they do not receive for their education any return from the taxes on the property. What is true of Georgia is true of every other Southern state. In 1904 the Superintendent of Public Instruction in North Carolina showed in his report that the Negroes were "in no danger of being given more than they were entitled to by every dictate of justice, right, wisdom, humanity, and Christianity."

In more recent years the principle of self-help has been especially exemplified in connection with the building of Rosenwald schools, which represent the co-operation of the Rosenwald Fund with the Negro people and the public-school authorities. By the close of 1936 these were 5,357 in number, and toward the total expense of $28,408,520 the Rosenwald Fund had contributed $4,366,519 and the Negro people themselves $4,725,871.

115. Self-Help in Collegiate Training. In higher education the principle of self-help has been best shown by the Baptist and Methodist denominations.

As we have seen, the educational work of the Negro Baptists was for a long time mainly under the direction of the American Baptist Home Mission Society. About the turn of the century, however, there was a widespread movement for independent work. This resulted in the founding of a large number of schools, about 125; and these ranged all the way from institutions doing college work to schools inadequately operated by small associations. As the public schools have advanced, most of these have been superseded; but we still have Selma University, Selma, Alabama; Arkansas Baptist College, Little Rock, Arkansas; Roger Williams-Howe College, Memphis, Tennessee; and the Virginia Theological Seminary and College, Lynchburg, Virginia.

Of the institutions of the African Methodist Episcopal Church, the foremost is Wilberforce University, Wilberforce, Ohio, but prominent also are Morris Brown University, Atlanta, Georgia; Allen University, Columbia, South Carolina; Paul Quinn College, Waco, Texas; and Kittrell College, Kittrell, North Carolina. Wilberforce was founded as early as 1856, but really entered on its career in 1863, when Bishop Daniel A. Payne made it the sole property of his denomination. This institution has fared better than others of the African Methodists, largely because some features of its work have assistance from the state of Ohio. The African Methodist Episcopal Zion Church is represented by Livingstone College, Salisbury, North Carolina. The Colored Methodist Episcopal Church has not as many schools as some other denominations, but in proportion to membership probably surpasses all other churches in exemplifying the principle of self-help. Its chief institutions are Lane College, Jackson, Tennessee; Miles Memorial College, Birmingham, Alabama; and the Mississippi Industrial College, Holly Springs, Mississippi. It also contributes to Paine College, Augusta, Georgia, operated by the Methodist Episcopal Church, South.

116. **Negro Philanthropy.** The Negro race is still comparatively poor, but already there have been many individuals who have given considerable sums to education or other worthy causes. Only a few can be mentioned. Thomy Lafon, of New Orleans, left $413,000 to charitable and educational institutions in that city, without distinction of color. John McKee, of Philadelphia, left at his death in 1902 about a million dollars in real estate for education. From the estate of Mary E. Shaw Tuskegee Institute received $38,000. George Washington, of Jerseyville, Illinois, left $15,000 for education; and in Baltimore Nancy Addison left $15,000 and Louis Bode $30,000 to the Community of Oblate Sisters of Providence. James D. Burrus, an alumnus of Fisk Uni-

versity, in 1928 left to his alma mater property amounting to $100,000; and in 1933 Dr. Lucy E. Moton, long principal of the institution that developed into Miner Teachers College, left $60,000 for the College of Medicine at Howard University.

CHAPTER XI

DISFRANCHISEMENT

117. Negro Suffrage before the Civil War. Our consideration of the founding of schools and colleges has taken us far beyond the immediate period we were discussing, that of Reconstruction; and in general we may observe that all effort in education aimed to adjust the freedman to the new day.

At the close of the chapter on enfranchisement we saw that a reaction had set in against liberalism, so much so that by 1879 large numbers of the Negro people felt impelled to leave the South altogether. This reactionary temper was dominant for the next quarter of a century, and in the period 1890-1910 one state after another enacted restrictive legislation.

This brings us to the large subject of disfranchisement; and in connection with it we may ask first of all, To what extent did the Negro have the suffrage in the United States before the Emancipation Proclamation? In answer we find that, at the time of the making of the Constitution, free men of the race could become voters in every one of the thirteen states except South Carolina and Georgia. Delaware, by an act of 1792, was the first of the other states to make discrimination. The other middle states followed her example, and in 1814 even Connecticut did likewise. At the time of the Civil

War disqualification had advanced so far that Negroes could vote only in five New England states and (under certain restrictions) in New York.[1]

118. The Sequel of Reconstruction. We have seen how the results of the Civil War were summed up in the Thirteenth Amendment, which abolished slavery, in the Fourteenth, which conferred citizenship on the former slaves, and in the Fifteenth, which protected them in the right to vote. Whatever may have been the faults of the Reconstruction era, so great was the lack of educational opportunity among the freedmen, and so speedy was the reaction against suffrage, that little accurate deduction could be drawn as to the real capacity of the former slave.

Nevertheless, the South soon decided not to try the experiment again if it could keep from doing so. In the decade 1870-1880, intimidation, theft or suppression of ballot boxes, removal of the polls to unknown places, false certifications, and illegal arrests on the day before an election were the chief means used to make the vote of the black man of no effect. Soon the Republican party in the South declined, and the Democrats refused to admit Negroes to their primaries. Generally after 1871 the vote of the freedman was in one way or another rendered ineffectual in every Southern state.

119. Changing Opinion. Such a situation is to be accounted for not only by matters pertaining to the Negro,

---

[1] A. B. Hart, *Negro Suffrage* (a contribution to the *Boston Evening Transcript*, March 24, 1906, reprinted as a pamphlet by the Niagara Movement).

but also by the larger forces at work in the life of the American people in the years following the war.

Again one might speak of "the decline of great convictions." After the spiritual elevation of the period of the war, the country, about 1870, descended into a period of industrialism, of opportunism, and even of dishonesty and scandal in high places. It was an age of materialism, not one of high principle; and in the stress of commercialism the Negro ceased to be an issue. The North was interested alike in new railroads in the West and mining and manufacturing in the South.

The era was signalized by one of the most effective speeches ever delivered in this or any other country, all the more forceful because the orator was a man of noble spirit. In 1886, just four nights before Christmas, Henry W. Grady, of Georgia, addressed the New England Club in New York on "The New South." He spoke to practical men and knew his ground. He asked his hearers to bring their "full faith in American fairness and frankness" to bear upon what he had to say. He pictured in brilliant language the Confederate soldier who, "ragged, half-starved, heavy-hearted," reached home only to find "his house in ruins, his farm devastated." He also spoke kindly of the Negro: "whenever he struck a blow for his own liberty, he fought in open battle, and when at last he raised his black and humble hands that the shackle might be struck off, those hands were innocent of wrong against his helpless charges." But Grady also implied that the Negro had received too much attention and sympathy from the North. Said he: "To liberty and enfranchisement is as far as the law can carry the Negro. The rest must be left to conscience and common sense." Hence he asked that the South be left alone in the handling of her grave problem.

The North, interested in its Southern investments, largely assented to this request, became more indifferent about the whole question of the Negro, and very soon there developed evils which Henry W. Grady, with his humanity, could certainly never have countenanced.

120. Peonage and Other Evils. One of the first of these evils to force attention was the peonage that was most frequently an outgrowth of the convict lease system. A noteworthy feature of legislation enacted in the South immediately after the Civil War was severe provision with reference to vagrancy. Negroes were often arrested on slight pretexts and their labor as that of convicts leased to landowners or other business men. When, moreover, Negroes, dissatisfied with their returns under the developing "share" system of labor, began a movement to the cities, there arose a tendency to make the vagrancy legislation still more harsh, so that often a laborer could not stop work without technically committing a crime. The abuses of the convict lease system at length arrested general attention, but meanwhile other evils had developed apace.

In the years about 1872 the number of Negroes lynched in the South is said to have been not more than eleven or twelve a year; but in 1892 the total number of victims lynched in the country was 255, the great majority being black men in the South. Within a period of thirty-five years not less than 3,200 Negro men and women were lynched within the boundaries of the

United States, and sometimes the burning or mutilation of the victims was savage in its brutality.

Moreover, separate and inferior traveling accommodations, meager provision for the education of children, inadequate street lighting, and water facilities in most cities and towns, and the lack of protection of life and property, especially in the rural districts, made life hard for the Negro people.

Nevertheless the Negroes made progress. By 1900 exactly 20 per cent of those in the Southern states were living in owned homes. In the decade ending with that year, they were still a considerable political factor in different communities of the South, as when in North Carolina a fusion of Republicans and Populists sent a Negro, George H. White, to Congress, thus defeating and alarming the Democrats. This incident, however, only served to strengthen the movement for disfranchisement that had already begun.

121. The Progress of Disfranchisement. However suppressed the Negro's vote may have been in actual practice, not until 1890 was he disfranchised in any state by direct legislation.

In this year the constitution of Mississippi was so amended as to exclude from the suffrage any person who had not paid his poll tax or was unable to read any section of the Constitution, or understand it when read to him, or to give a reasonable interpretation of it. The effect of the administration of this provision was to exclude the great majority of the Negroes. South Carolina amended her constitution with similar effect in 1895.

In 1898 Louisiana invented the so-called "grandfather

clause." This excused from the operation of her disfranchising act all descendants of men who had voted
before the Civil War, thus admitting to the suffrage all
white men who were illiterate and without property.

North Carolina in 1900, Virginia and Alabama in
1901, Georgia in 1907, and Oklahoma in 1910 in one way
or another practically disfranchised the Negro, care
being taken in each instance to avoid any deliberate
violation of the Fifteenth Amendment.

In Maryland there were various efforts to disfranchise
the Negro by constitutional amendments, one in 1905,
another in 1909, and still another in 1911; but all failed
by large majorities.

122. A Summary of the Legislation. However much
they may have differed in detail, the disfranchising acts
had three points in common: (a) Some device enabling
all white voters to evade the force of the new legislation; (b) the limiting clauses themselves; and (c) the
placing of sufficient discretionary power with boards
of registrars to enable them to act effectively.

In six of the disfranchising states—Louisiana, North
Carolina, Alabama, Virginia, Georgia, and Oklahoma—
"grandfather" clauses are in effect.

The amendment to the constitution of the state of
Georgia is fairly typical. In this state any male citizen
of legal age who has paid his poll tax may register and
vote if he can read accurately or write accurately a
paragraph of the state constitution that may be read to
him. Any person owning or paying taxes on $500 worth
of property may register and vote whether literate or
illiterate.

The provision that really eliminates the Negro is the common one to the effect that the registrars may use their discretion in determining what candidates for registration are of good character and understand the duties of citizenship.

123. Important Supreme Court Decisions. Naturally all such legislation as that just outlined had ultimately to be brought before the highest tribunal in the country.

The test came over the following section from the Oklahoma law: "No person shall be registered as an elector of this State or be allowed to vote in any election herein, unless he is able to read and write any section of the Constitution of the State of Oklahoma; but no person who was, on January 1, 1866, or at any time prior thereto, entitled to vote under any form of government, or who at any time resided in some foreign nation, and no lineal descendant of such person, shall be denied the right to register and vote because of his inability to so read and write sections of such Constitution." [2] This enactment the Supreme Court declared unconstitutional in 1915, but in some other tests the Negro did not fare so well.

A so-called White Primary Law, enacted in Texas in 1924 with the purpose of excluding Negroes from the Democratic primaries in the state, has received testing in court more than once; but the most important decision was that rendered by the Supreme Court of the United States April 1, 1935. R. R. Grovey, a Negro resident of Harris County, was denied the right to vote in the Democratic primary in 1934, and brought suit accord-

[2] *Constitution of Oklahoma*, Article III, Section 4a.

ingly. The Supreme Court, to which the case came at length, declared that the right to vote for one who is to hold public office must not be confused with the privilege of membership in a particular party, that the Democratic party in Texas was a voluntary political association, and that as such it had the power to determine who should be eligible for membership and participation in the party's primaries.

124. The Negro as a Political Force. Meanwhile it is to be observed that the Negro is not wholly without the vote even in the South; and in Chapter XV, "Recent History," will be seen something of the influence that he is able at times to exert. In the North moreover—especially in Indiana, Ohio, New Jersey, Illinois, Pennsylvania, and New York—he has power that on some occasions has proved to be a deciding factor.

Even when his suffrage is restricted, the Negro wields tremendous influence on the destinies of the nation, for, though some men may be disfranchised, *all* are counted in the allotment of congressmen to the southern states. In the presidential election of 1912 Massachusetts sent 18 electors to the electoral college and South Carolina 9; but for her 18 Massachusetts cast 488,156 votes, and for her 9 South Carolina cast 50,348. In 1914 Kansas and Mississippi each elected 8 members of the House of Representatives; but Kansas had to cast 483,683 votes for her members, while Mississippi cast only 37,185 for hers, less than one-twelfth as many. For the remedying of this situation by the enforcement of the Fourteenth Amendment so that representation shall be reduced in the proportion that the voting of adult male citizens is reduced, bills have frequently been presented in Congress; but so far no definite action has been taken. Some thoughtful Negroes oppose such action on principle, feeling that it would permanently make for a submerged group, and that the Negro will finally arrive at his full estate in the councils of the nation not by such radical means but by the quiet leverage of educational **and** economic progress.

CHAPTER XII

THE TUSKEGEE IDEA

125. Hampton Institute. Hampton Normal and Agricultural Institute was opened in April, 1868, under the auspices of the American Missionary Association, with General Samuel Chapman Armstrong in charge. In 1870 it was chartered by a special act of the General Assembly of Virginia and thus became independent.

The aim of the school was expressed by the founder in these words: "to train selected Negro youth who should go out and teach and lead their people, first by example by getting land and homes; to give them not a dollar that they can earn for themselves; to teach respect for labor; to replace stupid drudgery with skilled hands; and to these ends to build up an industrial system for the sake not only of self-support and intelligent labor, but also for the sake of character." [1]

On the Institute grounds there are 139 buildings, these ranging all the way from the large Ogden Auditorium to small frame structures; and at Shellbanks, four miles distant, there are 11 buildings, several of which were erected by student labor. The home farm contains 96 acres and the one at Shellbanks 820.

There is a flourishing summer school, and important

[1] General Samuel C. Armstrong, "The Founding of Hampton Institute," *Old South Leaflets*, VI, No. 149, 521.

conferences are held from time to time. About 1920 Hampton embarked upon a comprehensive reorganization of its work and the establishment of schools offering courses for the degree of Bachelor of Science. In 1937-1938 the collegiate enrollment was 1,019, and the figure for all schools and departments was 2,354.

The practical nature of the work at Hampton, the military discipline, the opportunity for technical education, and the beauty of the location have made the institution deservedly famous.

126. The Time and the Man. Here then at Hampton Institute was developing a marvelous equipment, with emphasis on matters of daily interest and concern. Hardly anyone realized in 1880 how much the sort of training here given was in accord with the industrial spirit so soon to be potent in the South. For a decade young men and women had been sent forth with the message of cleaner and thriftier living; but their activity had been confined almost wholly to Virginia. What was needed was for some strong man to go down to the cotton belt, interpret the lesson for the men and women digging in the ground, teach them better methods, and generally place them in line with the South's development. The man was ready in the person of one of Hampton's own graduates.

127. Booker T. Washington. Booker Taliaferro Washington was born in Franklin County, Virginia, April 5, 1856. After the Civil War his mother and stepfather went to Malden, West Virginia, where in his boyhood he worked in the salt furnaces and coal mines. He had always been called Booker, but it was not until he went to a little school at his home and found that he needed a surname that on the spur of the moment he adopted *Washington*. Later he learned that the surname was really *Taliaferro*, and he took this as his middle name. In 1872 he worked his way to Hampton Institute, where he paid his expenses in part by assisting as a janitor. Graduating in 1875, he returned to Malden and taught school for three years. He then attended for a year Wayland Seminary in Washington (now incorporated in Virginia Union University in Richmond), and in 1879 was appointed an instructor at Hampton. In 1881 there came to General Armstrong a call from the little town of Tuskegee, Alabama, for some one to organize and become the principal of a normal school that the people wanted to start in the town. He recommended Mr. Washington, who opened the school on the 4th of July in an old church and a little shanty, with an attendance of thirty pupils. In 1895 Mr. Washington came into national prominence by a remarkable speech at the Cotton States Exposition in Atlanta, and later he interested educators generally by his emphasis on practical education. In 1896 the degree of Master of Arts was conferred on him by Harvard University, and that of Doctor of Laws by Dartmouth in 1901. He died November 14, 1915.

128. **Message to the South.** The message which this man brought to the South, both to his own and to the white people, may best be expressed in his own words at the Atlanta Exposition: "To those of my race who depend on bettering their condition in a foreign land, or who underestimate the importance of cultivating

PROFESSOR GEORGE WASHINGTON CARVER OF TUSKEGEE, FOR
HALF A CENTURY A TRAIL BLAZER IN INDUSTRIAL RESEARCH ON
FARM PRODUCTS

friendly relations with the Southern white man who is their next-door neighbor, I would say: 'Cast down your bucket where you are'—cast it down in making friends, in every manly way, of the people of all races by whom we are surrounded. . . . To those of the white race who look to the incoming of those of foreign birth and strange tongue and habits for the prosperity of the South, were I permitted, I would repeat what I say to my race, 'Cast down your bucket where you are.' Cast it down among the eight million Negroes whose habits you know, whose fidelity and love you have tested in days when to have proved treacherous meant the ruin of your firesides. . . . In all things that are purely social we can be as separate as the fingers, yet one as the hand in all things essential to mutual progress." [2]

129. **Significant Utterances.** A few sentences from the speeches of Dr. Washington may serve further to give an idea of his teaching and his gospel work. Said he:

"Freedom can never be given. It must be purchased." [3] "The race, like the individual, that makes itself indispensable, has solved most of its problems." [3] "As a race there are two things we must learn to do—one is to put brains and skill into the common occupations of life, and the other is to dignify common labor." [4] "Ignorant and inexperienced, it is not strange that in the first years of our new life we began at the top instead of at the bottom; that a seat in Congress or the State Legislature was more sought than real estate or industrial skill." [5]

[2] Speech at Atlanta Exposition, September 18, 1895.
[3] Speech before N. E. A. in St. Louis, June 30, 1904.
[4] Speech at Fisk University, 1895.
[5] Speech at Atlanta Exposition, September 18, 1895.

"The opportunity to earn a dollar in a factory just now is worth infinitely more than the opportunity to spend a dollar in an opera house." [6]

He asserted, "one of the most vital questions that touches our American life is how to bring the strong, wealthy, and learned into helpful contact with the poorest, most ignorant, and humblest, and at the same time make the one appreciate the vitalizing, strengthening influence of the other." [7] "There is no defense or security for any of us except in the highest intelligence and development of all." [6]

130. Tuskegee Institute.   Dr. Washington's views about industrial education and the importance of the Negro's making himself respected found expression in Tuskegee Normal and Industrial Institute. Beginning in 1881 with one teacher and an annual grant of only $2,000 from the Alabama Legislature, the institution organized a college soon after the World War, and in 1937-1938 enrolled in all schools and departments 2,177 students, of whom 1,160 were doing college work. There are on the grounds more than 130 buildings, erected largely by student labor; and not less than 40 industries have been operated.

One of the important features of the work is the activity of the Extension Division. At one time or another this has included an annual Negro conference, monthly institutes for farmers, short courses in agriculture, farm demonstration work, a town night school, the County Institute, the Ministers' Night School,

[6] Speech at Atlanta Exposition, September 18, 1895.
[7] Speech at Harvard University, June 24, 1896.

mothers' meetings, a state and county fair, and a special conference on the Negro as a World Problem.

Within recent years, in view of the advance of machinery in the United States, Tuskegee has had to reconsider its emphasis on hand labor, so that just now the institution is in a large way in a state of reorganization and of adjustment to the new day.

131. Offshoots. The importance of the general idea becomes manifest when it is realized that Tuskegee itself is not the only institution in the far South that was founded to emphasize practical training for the Negro. More than fifteen schools with a similar aim have been established by graduates. These are widely scattered, but typical ones are the Voorhees Industrial School, Denmark, South Carolina; the Robert Hungerford School, Eatonville, Florida; the Snow Hill Normal and Industrial Institute, Snow Hill, Alabama; the Utica Normal and Industrial Institute, Utica, Mississippi; the Port Royal Agricultural School, Beaufort, South Carolina; and the Mt. Meigs Institute, Mt. Meigs, Alabama.

132. The National Negro Business League. One typical organization will illustrate the influence of the Tuskegee idea. The National Negro Business League, of which Dr. Washington was the founder and the first president, is not officially connected with the Institute; but it was conceived in the spirit of that institution and has adhered to its line of work. It was organized in 1899, and within a few years there were scores of local leagues scattered throughout the country.

When this organization began work, there were hardly more than half a dozen Negro banks in the

United States. In 1938 there were 23, aside from building and loan societies and mutual savings associations. Stores and industrial enterprises to the number of 20,000 came into existence, and some remarkable stories of the growth of thrift and industry among his people were told by Dr. Washington in *The Negro in Business* and others of his books.

Of course much of this progress would have been realized if the National Negro Business League had never been organized, but it is clear that a vital moving force in this field of development was the genius of the leader at Tuskegee.

CHAPTER XIII

VIOLENCE AND SOCIAL UNREST

133. Mob Violence. The two decades immediately following 1890, the year in which disfranchisement began, form a period of singular stress in the history of the Negro in America. In the reaction against Reconstruction there was not only proscription but defamation. The white South was again in control, but predictions for a broader outlook were not yet fulfilled, and the time became one of bitter social antagonism.

If the black man's labor was to be exploited, it was necessary that he be without political power and that he be denied justice in court. Accordingly there developed everywhere the idea of inferior service for Negroes, and a brutal prison system flourished in all its hideousness. Now arose as never before the form of the Negro criminal; and some writers were led to lament the passing of slavery and to point cynically to the effects of freedom. They failed to remember in the case of the criminal that from childhood to manhood —in education, in economic chance, in legal power— they had deprived a human being of what was due him; and then they were aghast at the thing their hands had made.

Lynching rose to such heights as the country had never known before In the month of February, 1893, the average was almost one a day. The cause most frequently alleged was that of a crime against womanhood; but statistics over a period of thirty years showed that this did not figure in more than 30 per cent of the cases recorded. More common was the crime of murder, and this frequently grew out of a dispute arising over work or wages. Near the close of 1894, in Brooks County, Georgia, after a Negro named Pike had killed a white man with whom he had a quarrel, seven Negroes were lynched after the real murderer escaped. On one Sunday in October, 1898, the country recorded two race wars, one lynching, two murders, one of which was expected to lead to a lynching, with a total of ten Negroes killed and four wounded, and four white men killed and seven wounded. In not a single case was the honor of womanhood involved. Walter Hines Page, writing in the *Forum* (December, 1893) on "The Last Hold of the Southern Bully," said of lynching: "The great danger is not in the first violation of law, nor in the crime itself, but in the danger that southern public sentiment under the stress of this phase of the race problem will lose the true perspective of civilization."

134. Election Troubles. Wilmington. The temper of the decade was shown especially in the events centering around some elections.

At Phoenix, in Greenwood County, South Carolina, on November 8, 1898, and for some days thereafter, the Tolberts, a well-known family of white Republicans, were attacked by mobs and barely escaped alive. R. R. Tolbert was a candidate for Congress. On election day his brother, Thomas Tolbert, was taking the affidavits

of Negroes who were not permitted to vote in order
that the election might be contested. While thus engaged
he was attacked by Etheridge, the Democratic manager
of another precinct. The Negroes came to Tolbert's
defense, and in the fight that followed Etheridge was
killed and Tolbert wounded. John Tolbert, father of
the family, coming up, was filled with buckshot, and a
younger member of the family was also hurt. All told
it appears that two white men and not less than twelve
Negroes lost their lives in connection with the trouble,
six of the latter being lynched on account of the death
of Etheridge.

About the same time there were serious disorders
in a neighboring state. In North Carolina, in 1894, the
Republicans by combining with the Populists had gained
control of the state legislature. In 1896 the Democrats
were again outvoted, and several local offices in the
state were in the hands of Negroes. Before the election
in November, 1898, the Democrats in Wilmington announced their determination to prevent Negroes from
holding office in that city. They had been made angry
by a local Negro paper, the *Record*, whose editor, A. L.
Manly, had replied sharply to a prominent woman of
the South who had recently spoken in Georgia defending lynching in certain cases. Election day itself passed
without disturbance, the streets being patrolled by
Democrats wearing red shirts; but on the next day there
was a mass meeting of the white citizens, at which there
was adopted a resolution to banish the editor of the
Record; and a committee of twenty-five was appointed
to see that this was done within twenty-four hours. In

the course of the day that followed, the printing office was destroyed, several white Republicans were driven from the city, and nine Negroes were killed at once, though no one could say just how many more lost their lives before the trouble was over. Charles W. Chesnutt, in *The Marrow of Tradition*, has given a portrayal of these events, the Wellington of the story being Wilmington. How the occurrence was regarded by a Southern minister may be seen from the words of A. J. McKelway, a Presbyterian editor, who wrote articles for the *Independent* and the *Outlook* justifying the proceedings. Said he: "It is difficult to speak of the Red Shirts without a smile. They victimized the Negroes with a huge practical joke. A dozen men would meet at a crossroad, on horseback, clad in red shirts of calico, flannel or silk, according to the taste of the owner and the enthusiasm of his womankind. They would gallop through the country, and the Negro would quietly make up his mind that his interest in political affairs was not a large one, anyway." It thus appears that the forcible seizure of the political rights of a large number of people, and the killing or wounding of many, amounted in the eyes of some to not more than a "practical joke."

135. The Atlanta Massacre. The disorders continued even as a new century dawned. On the night of March 15, 1899, in Palmetto, Georgia, several Negroes who were thought to have connections with some fires in the town, were confined in a low, close warehouse to await trial the next day. About midnight a mob came, pushed open the door, and fired two volleys at the men, killing four instantly and fatally wounding four more.

Less than six weeks later, on Sunday, April 23, at New-nan, not far away, occurred one of the most notorious of all lynchings, that of Sam Hose, the burning being preceded by mutilation. In July, 1900, in New Orleans, a Negro, Robert Charles, offered some variation in the current trend, startling the country by the dearness with which he sold his life. He had committed no crime, but wounded an officer in resisting arrest. Barricading himself in a two-story house, he killed eight of his assail-ants and wounded two or three more before he was slain. In the same year, on the night of August 15, there were serious riots in the city of New York. In March, 1904, near Doddsville, Mississippi, occurred the so-called "corkscrew lynching," a Negro, Luther Holbert, accused of murdering his employer, and his innocent wife both being subjected to gross torture before they were burned.

The real climax of violence in the period, however, was the Atlanta Massacre of Saturday, September 22, 1906. This was an outgrowth of the heated campaign of Hoke Smith for the governorship. Throughout the summer sentiment for the disfranchisement of the Negro was capitalized, and lurid stories about Negroes were built up in an afternoon paper. Early Saturday night, in the heart of the city, some elements, heated by liquor and newspaper extras, became openly riotous and defied all authority. Negroes were assaulted wherever they appeared; in one barber shop two workers were beaten to death and their bodies mangled. In all nearly a score of persons lost their lives, and many more were injured. Sunday dawned upon a city of astounded white people

and outraged and sullen Negroes. Throughout Monday and Tuesday the tension continued. On Monday night, when some citizens joined policemen in advancing on a suburb of Negro homes, one officer was killed, and some of those with him were wounded. More Negroes were also killed, but it was this disposition to make armed resistance that really put an end to the massacre.

136. Individual Achievement. It seems a far cry from such events as these to the worthy achievements of individual Negroes; yet nothing is more true in the history of the Negro than that sorrow and success often go together. At the very time that the race was being discounted and defamed, there arose here and there persons who were in themselves the refutation of all that was said.

In 1895, the year in which Booker T. Washington spoke in Atlanta, a young man of Negro descent, W. E. Burghardt DuBois, received the degree of Doctor of Philosophy at Harvard. There had been sound scholars in the race before DuBois, but here was a thorough student in the new field of economics, one able to approach the problems of his people on the basis of modern science, and he was destined to do great good.

The next year an authentic young poet who had wrestled with poverty and doubt at last gained a hearing, for it was then that Paul Laurence Dunbar published through Dodd, Mead and Company his *Lyrics of Lowly Life*.

In 1896 also, a young Negro American painter, Henry O. Tanner, began to win laurels in Paris.

From abroad came word of one musician, Samuel

Coleridge-Taylor, who in 1898, with *Hiawatha's Wedding-Feast*, entered the rank of the foremost living English composers. In 1894 Harry T. Burleigh, competing against sixty candidates, became baritone soloist at St. George's Episcopal Church, New York. At the same time Madame Sissieretta Jones was giving new proof of the possibilities of the Negro as an artist in song. In the previous decade Madame Marie Selika had delighted audiences in both America and Europe, and in 1887 had appeared Flora Batson, whose ballad singing often moved her hearers to the wildest enthusiasm.

137. The Spanish-American War. Outstanding in the course of the decade was the work of the Negro soldier in the Spanish-American War.

There were at the time four regiments of colored regulars in the Army of the United States, the Twenty-fourth Infantry, the Twenty-fifth Infantry, the Ninth Cavalry, and the Tenth Cavalry; and colored troops enlisted in the volunteer service in Massachusetts, Indiana, Illinois, Kansas, Ohio, North Carolina, Tennessee, and Virginia. The Eighth Illinois was officered throughout by Negroes, J. R. Marshall commanding; and Major Charles Young, a West Point graduate, was in charge of the Ohio battalion.

The very first regiment ordered to the front when the war broke out was the Twenty-fourth Infantry; and Negro troops were conspicuous in the fighting around Santiago. They figured in a brilliant charge at Las Quasimas on June 24, 1898; and in an attack on July 1 at El Caney, a mile and a half from Santiago, the First Volunteer Cavalry (Colonel Theodore Roosevelt's "Rough Riders") was saved from annihilation by the gallant work of the men of the Tenth Cavalry. Fully as patriotic, though in another way, was a deed of the Twenty-fourth Infantry. Learning that General Nelson A. Miles desired men for the cleaning of a yellow-fever hospital and the nursing of some victims of the disease, this regiment offered its services and by one day's work so cleared away the rubbish and cleaned the camp that the number of cases was greatly reduced.

Said the *Review of Reviews* in editorial comment (October, 1898): "One of the most gratifying incidents of the Spanish War has been the enthusiasm that the colored regiments of the regular army have aroused throughout the whole country. Their fighting at Santiago was magnificent. The Negro soldiers showed excellent discipline, the highest qualities of personal bravery, very superior physical endurance, unfailing good temper, and the most generous disposition toward all comrades in arms, whether white or black. Roosevelt's Rough Riders have come back singing the praises of the colored troops. There is not a dissenting voice in the chorus of praise."

138. Brownsville. After this record in the war with Spain, the criticism that the Negro soldier was called on to bear within the period was all the more hard to accept.

In August, 1906, Companies B, C, and D of the Twenty-fifth Regiment, United States Infantry, were stationed at Fort Brown, Brownsville, Texas, where they were forced to exercise great self-restraint in the face of daily insults from the citizens. On the night of August

13 occurred a riot in which one citizen was killed, another wounded, and the chief of police injured. The people of the town accused the soldiers of causing the riot and demanded their removal. The Inspector General was sent to find the guilty men, and, failing in his mission, he recommended dishonorable discharge for the regiment. On this recommendation, President Theodore Roosevelt on November 9 dismissed "without honor" the entire battalion, disqualifying its members for service thereafter in either the military or the civil employ of the United States.

When Congress met in December Senator Joseph B. Foraker of Ohio placed himself at the head of the critics of the President's action, and in a ringing speech he said of the discharged men, "They ask no favors because they are Negroes, but only justice because they are men." On January 22, 1907, the Senate authorized an investigation of the whole matter, a special message from the President on January 14 having revoked the civil disability of the discharged soldiers. The case was finally disposed of by a congressional act approved March 3, 1909, which appointed a court of inquiry before which any one of the men who wished to reenlist had the burden of establishing his innocence—a procedure which clearly violated the fundamental principle in law that a man is to be accounted innocent until he is proved guilty.

139. The New Question of Labor. It was also in this period that the question of organized labor came forward as never before. In March, 1895, there were bloody riots in New Orleans, growing out of the fact that white laborers who were beginning to be organized objected to the employment of Negroes for the unloading of vessels. Early in August of this year there were conflicts between the white and the black miners in Birmingham, a number being killed on both sides before military authority could intervene. All such events brought into sharp relief the struggle between capital and labor, and there was naturally wide difference of opinion.

The real climax of labor trouble as of mob violence within the period came in Georgia and in Atlanta, a city that now assumed importance as a battleground of the problems of the New South. In April, 1909, ten white workers on the Georgia Railroad who had been placed on the "extra list" were replaced by Negroes at lower wages. Against this there was violent protest all along the route. A little later the white Firemen's Union started a strike that intended ultimately to drive all Negro firemen from Southern roads. In the struggle that ensued not all of the newspapers in the South approved the attitude of the white firemen; thus the Baltimore *News* said, "If the Negro can be driven from one skilled employment, he can be driven from another; but a country that tries to do it is flying in the face of every economic law, and must feel the evil effects of its policy if it could be carried out." At any rate feeling ran high; for a whole week about June 1 there were very few trains between Atlanta and Augusta, and there were some acts of violence; but in view of the capital at stake, the owners of the railroad felt that they could not retreat. A board of arbitration ultimately decided that the Georgia Railroad was still to employ Negroes when they were found qualified, and that such men were to receive the same wages as white workers. Some thought that this decision would ultimately tell against the Negro, but such was not the immediate effect. The whole matter was in fact one of the most pathetic we have had to record. Humble white workers, desiring to improve their condition, instead of assuming a statesmanlike attitude toward their problem, turned aside into the wilderness of racial hatred, and were lost.

140. Conflicting Opinion. In view of the mob violence, the disfranchisement, and the proscription it was but natural that thoughtful Negro men should have some difference of opinion as to the best way for their people to advance.

The program advanced by Booker T. Washington at once commanded attention; both the North and the South approved the new leader, and he certainly gave inspiration to thousands of his fellowmen.

From the first, however, there was a group of Negro men who questioned the ultimate wisdom of the so-called Atlanta Compromise. They felt that in being willing even temporarily to accept segregation and to waive political rights Dr. Washington had given up too much. It happened that at first they were not united and that their utterance sometimes offended by harshness of tone. Dr. Washington himself said of the extremists in this group that they frequently understood theories but not things; that in college they gave little thought to preparing for any definite work in the world, but started out with the idea of solving the race problem;

and that many of them made a business of keeping the
wrongs and hardships of the Negro people before the
public.[1] There was ample ground for his criticism; at
the same time there was some virtue in the other point
of view. To some extent the contest was the old one
between the realist and the idealist. The *Guardian*, edited
in Boston by Monroe Trotter, was particularly out-
spoken; the *Voice of the Negro*, a monthly magazine
published for three years in Atlanta, helped with earnest
thinking; and, by reason of a chapter in *The Souls of
Black Folk*, Dr. DuBois became known as the chief
critic of the powerful leader at Tuskegee.

141. The Niagara Movement. In 1905 the opposition
to Booker T. Washington's program crystallized in organization. Twenty-nine Negro leaders launched what
was known, from their meeting place, as the Niagara
Movement. The aims of the organization were freedom
of speech and criticism, an unsubsidized press, manhood
suffrage, the abolition of distinctions based simply on
race and color, the recognition of the principle of human
brotherhood as a practical present creed, the recognition
of the highest training as the monopoly of no class or
race, a belief in the dignity of labor, and united effort
to realize these ideals under wise and courageous leadership. The time was not yet ripe, and the Niagara
Movement, as such, died after three or four years. Its
principles lived on, however, and its leading spirit, Dr.
DuBois, became identified with a new and stronger

[1] See Booker T. Washington, *My Larger Education* (New York:
Doubleday Page & Co., 1909), chapter on "The Intellectuals."

Photo from The Scurlock Studio

W. E. BURGHARDT DUBOIS, NOTED AUTHOR

organization, the National Association for the Advancement of Colored People, which was more successful.

142. The National Association for the Advancement of Colored People. This Association for which Dr. DuBois became Director of Publicity and Research in 1910, was begun by a group of men and women, without distinction as to race, who were so interested in the welfare of the Negro and the principles on which the country was founded that they felt that the time had come for a simple declaration of human rights.

The organization announced that it aimed "to make 11,000,000 Americans physically free from peonage, mentally free from ignorance, politically free from disfranchisement, and socially free from insult." It soon reached a membership of 100,000, its organ being the *Crisis*, a monthly periodical issued in New York, with Dr. DuBois as editor (until 1934). It wages a constant fight for justice in every way, has won some important court decisions, and has been especially successful in placing before the public the evils of lynching.

Much of the success of such effort is to be credited to Moorfield Storey, once secretary to Charles Sumner, who served as president of the organization until his death in 1930; to the late Louis Marshall, distinguished lawyer, long a member of the Board of Directors; to Dr. Joel E. Spingarn, treasurer and later president; to Arthur B. Spingarn, vice-president and chairman of the Legal Committee; to James Weldon Johnson, who served for some years as secretary, and to Walter White, the alert secretary in recent years.

143. The National Urban League. The work of the National Association for the Advancement of Colored People was admirably complemented by that of another organization formed about the same time, the National Urban League. This has been concerned primarily with the economic life of the Negro, and it has as its motto, "Not alms, but opportunity."

In 1909 Mrs. Ruth Standish Baldwin, whose husband had served as a trustee of Tuskegee Institute, called together at her home a number of leaders of both races to discuss the social problems of the Negro in the metropolis. This was the beginning of an organization that by its twenty-fifth anniversary had local leagues in not less than forty-three cities.

The National Urban League was interested from the first in the cases of Negro children who appeared before juvenile courts; it succeeded in placing the first regular Negro internes in a municipal hospital; and it secured the appointment of Negro personnel workers in industrial plants at the time of the World War. Through such departments as those of Industrial Relations and of Research and Investigation, it has conducted its special activities; and fellowships granted to advanced students interested in social work have averaged a little more than three a year. A monthly magazine, *Opportunity*, has also given encouragement to Negro writers and artists; for some years it fostered the Holstein Literary Prize contests.

The executive secretary of the National Urban League for practically the whole period of its existence has been **Dr.** Eugene Kinckle Jones.

144. Efforts for Better Understanding. In the far South also there was effort for a better social order, in spite of much that was discouraging.

In May, 1900, there was in Montgomery, Alabama, a conference in which Southern men undertook as never before to make a study of their problems. Some of those who attended were reactionary in temper, and others had no real conception of the task before them; but there were also those who had the vision of statesmen. William A. McCorkle, a former governor of West Virginia, said that the right of franchise was the vital and underlying principle of the life of the people of the United States and must not be violated, that the remedy for present conditions was an "honest and inflexible educational and property basis, administered fairly for black and white," and that the Negro problem was not a local problem but one to be settled by the hearty co-operation of all the people of the nation.

About the same time the efforts of a group of forward-looking men created new interest in education; and, especially after Dr. J. H. Dillard became president of the Jeanes Fund, young men in college showed increasing concern about their highest duty as patriots. Phelps-Stokes fellowships for the study of problems relating to the Negro were founded at representative universities, and in 1912 the University Commission on Southern Race Questions was organized.

Of unusual significance has been the work of the Commission on Interracial Cooperation, which now has numerous branches and which insists that in every community in which there are questions affecting the races, thinking people of both groups shall labor to the end that a Christian solution may be found.

In very recent years there has been established the Association of Southern Women for the Prevention of Lynching.

More and more it appears that an enlightened spirit is abroad in the land.

CHAPTER XIV

THE WORLD WAR AND THE NEGRO

145. The Policy of the Wilson Administrations. In view of some of the things that had happened in the early years of the century, when the Republicans were still ascendant in the nation, Negro men were led to wonder about their traditional allegiance to that party, and many looked with hope to the change of government in 1913 that brought Woodrow Wilson into office.

Before the election, on October 16, 1912, in speaking of the Negro people, Mr. Wilson had said: "Should I become President of the United States, they may count on me for absolute fair dealing and for everything by which I could assist in advancing the interests of their race in the United States." This promise was destined not to be fulfilled. Within a few months prominent Negro officials were removed in the Post-office and Treasury Departments, and it became clear that there was at work a policy either to segregate Negro workers in the Federal service and restrict them in the main to menial positions, or to eliminate them altogether.

In speaking to the University Commission on Southern Race Questions about the problems of the South, the President said that it was necessary to help the Negro along "sensible" lines. The black man had learned to be dubious about any such special provision, and he was fated to have even more reason for concern in the years of the World War as to the outcome of this policy.

146. Carrizal.   Suddenly, in June, 1916, the American people were again impressed by the loyalty and heroism of the Negro soldier. The expedition of American forces into Mexico in this month, with the political events attending this, is a long story; but the outstanding incident was that in which two troops of the Tenth Cavalry were engaged.

Said the *Review of Reviews* in reporting the matter: "The unfortunate occurrence at Carrizal, on June 21 . . . involves questions of fact upon which we are not prepared to express an opinion. About eighty colored troopers from the Tenth Cavalry had been sent a long distance away from the main line of the American army, on some such ostensible errand as the pursuit of a deserter. The situation being as it was, it might well seem that this venture was highly imprudent. At or near the town of Carrizal, our men seem to have chosen to go through the town rather than around it, and the result was a clash which resulted in the death of Captain Boyd, who commanded the detachment, and some twenty of his men, twenty-two others being taken prisoners by the Mexicans. According to Mexican accounts, our troops made the attack; according to reports of our own men, the Mexicans set a trap and opened fire. Meanwhile all other phases of the Mexican problem seemed for the moment to have been forgotten at Washington in the demand for the release of the twenty-two men who had been captured. There was of course no reason for holding them, and they were brought to El Paso within a few days and sent across the line." [1]

Thus, though "someone had blundered," the men did their duty, fighting in the face of odds and once more giving proof of their valor.

147. Migration. Soon after the beginning of the war in Europe in 1914, there began what may ultimately be known as the most notable of all the migrations of the Negro in America.

The ceasing of the stream of immigration from Europe created an unprecedented demand for labor in the industrial centers of the North, and business men turned to a source that had as yet been used in only slight degree. Special agents worked to some degree, but the outstanding feature of the new migration was that it was primarily a mass movement and not one organized or encouraged by any group of leaders. Those who left their homes in the South to find new ones in the North worked in response to an economic demand, but prominent among the forces that urged them on was the thought of the generally unsatisfactory conditions in the section from which they came.

It is a conservative estimate to say that in the four-year period 1915-1918 not less than 500,000 Negroes thus changed their place of abode. Naturally in such a number were many ignorant persons, but sometimes those who sold their property and moved away were skilled artisans and the most stable element in their communities

[1] "The Carrizal Occurrence," *Review of Reviews*, LIV, No. 2 (August, 1916), 134.

148. Economic Adjustment: East St. Louis. With such a shifting of population it was but to be expected that there would be some inconvenience and hardship. In Pittsburgh and Philadelphia congestion in housing became so great as to force immediate attention. Here and there were outbreaks in which lives were lost. The whole problem of the Negro laborer was of such commanding importance after the United States entered the war as to lead to the creation of a special Division of Negro Economics in the office of the Secretary of Labor. To the directorship of this was called Dr. George E. Haynes, formerly a professor at Fisk University.

The most serious of the outbreaks was that in East St. Louis, Illinois, where the feeling led to one of the most depressing occurrences in the whole history of the race in America. For years this city had been an important industrial center. In the summer of 1915 a strike on the part of 4,500 white men in the packing plants moved the owners to call in Negroes from the South, and by the spring of the next year perhaps as many as 10,000 had recently arrived in the city. Riots took place as early as May, and on July 2 there began a massacre in which hundreds of thousands of dollars in property were destroyed, 6,000 Negroes driven from their homes, and about 150 shot, burned, hanged, or maimed for life. Officers of the law failed to do their duty, and the testimony of victims as to the torture inflicted upon them was such as to send a thrill of horror through the hearts of the American people.

There was unrest in other places, but different organizations labored earnestly to adjust the Negro to his new environment. Representative was the Detroit branch of the National Urban League. This agency was not content simply to find vacant positions, but approached the managers of numerous establishments with a tactful and forceful appeal, and within twelve months placed not less than a thousand Negroes in employment other than unskilled labor.

149. Camp Dodge.   When the United States entered the World War in April, 1917, the question of overwhelming importance to the Negro people was naturally that of their relation to the great conflict in which their country had become engaged. Their response to the draft call set a notable example of loyalty.

At the very outset the race faced a dilemma over a separate training camp for Negro officers that the Government seemed disposed to establish. If there were to be training camps for officers, and if the Government would make no provision otherwise, did it wish to have a special camp for Negroes, such as would give formal approval to a policy of segregation, or did it wish to have no camp at all on such terms and thus have none of the younger men of the race trained as officers? Dr. Joel E. Spingarn, of the National Association for the Advancement of Colored People, took the lead in moulding sentiment for the camp; it was secured—Camp Dodge, near Des Moines, Iowa; and throughout the summer of 1917 the work of training went forward, the heart of a harassed and burdened people responding more and more with pride to the work of their men. On October 15, 625 became commissioned officers, and 1,200 in all received commissions.

For the fighting forces of the United States the **Negro** race furnished nearly 400,000 men, of whom just a little more than half actually saw service in Europe.

150. The Negro in the War. Negro men saw service in all branches of the military establishment, except that they were not formally in aviation.

For the handling of many of the problems relating to them Emmett J. Scott was on October 1, 1917, appointed Special Assistant to the Secretary of War. Mr. Scott had for a number of years been associated with Booker T. Washington as secretary, and in 1909 he was one of the three members of the commission appointed by President Taft for the investigation of Liberian affairs.

Negro nurses were placed in the base hospitals at six army camps, and Negro women served also as canteen workers in France and as hostesses for the camps at home. Service of signal value was rendered by Negro women in industry, and it was the women also who largely maintained and promoted the food supply at the same time that they released men for duty at the front.

In the summer of 1918 interest naturally centered upon the performance of the soldiers in France and upon the establishment of units of the Students' Army Training Corps in twenty educational institutions. Sixty Negro men served as chaplains and 350 as Y. M. C. A. secretaries.

Negro soldiers fought with distinction in the Argonne Forest, in the Vosges Mountains, in the St. Mihiel district, in the Champagne sector, and at Metz, often winning the highest praise from their commanders. Entire regiments were cited for valor and decorated with the

Croix de Guerre—the 369th, the 371st, and the 372nd; and groups of officers and men of the 365th, the 366th, the 368th, the 370th, and the first battalion of the 367th were also decorated.

The 370th was the first American regiment stationed in the St. Mihiel sector; it was one of three that occupied a sector at Verdun when a penetration there would have been disastrous to the Allies; and it had been sent straight from the training camp to the firing-line. Notable also was the record of the 369th Infantry, formerly the Fifteenth Regiment, New York National Guard. This organization was under shellfire for 191 days, and it held one trench for 91 days without relief. It was the first unit of the Allies to reach the Rhine, going down as an advance guard of the French army of occupation. Hardly less heroic was the service of the stevedore regiments, that sometimes had to work under terrific pressure. General Vincenden said of the men of the 370th: "Fired by a noble ardor, they go at times beyond the objectives given them by the higher command; they have always wished to be in the front line"; and General Gobyet said of the 371st and 372nd: "The most powerful defenses, the most strongly organized machine-gun nests, the heaviest artillery barrages—nothing could stop them. These crack regiments overcame every obstacle with a most complete contempt for danger. They have shown us the way to victory."

At the close of the war the highest Negro officers in the army were Lieutenant Colonel Otis B. Duncan, commander of the third battalion of the 370th, formerly the Eighth Illinois, and the highest ranking Negro officer in the American Expeditionary Forces; Colonel Charles Young, retired but on special duty at Camp Grant, Illinois; Colonel Franklin A. Dennison, of the 370th Infantry; and Lieutenant Colonel Benjamin O. Davis, of the Ninth Cavalry.

151. Individual Heroism.   Individual citations for gallantry in action were many, but only a few can be mentioned.

Henry Johnson and Needham Roberts, of the 369th, were the first men in the ranks of all the American Expeditionary Forces to receive the Croix de Guerre. They figured in a remarkable exploit before day on May 14, 1918, when they repelled a party of more than twenty Germans that raided the post at which they were stationed.

While the 368th was in the Argonne, John Baker, of Company I, volunteered one day to take a message to another part of the line. A shell struck his hand, tearing away part of it, but he went on his way without stopping. On another occasion it was necessary to send a runner from the same company across a field swept by fire. Edward Saunders responded to the call, but he had not gone far before a shell struck him down. He called to his comrades for someone to come and get the message. Lieutenant Robert L. Campbell dashed across the field, picked up the wounded·man, and carried him to safety. Both were cited for the Distinguished Service Cross, and Campbell, in addition, was recommended for a captaincy. T. Edward Jones, a first lieutenant in the medical corps attached to this same regiment, the 368th, went out when a man was gravely wounded, and, not

waiting for the stretcher-bearers and being unable himself to move the man, performed an emergency operation
under fire. He too later became a captain and was given
the Distinguished Service Cross.

For their work in breaking up machine-gun nests on
two successive days, Corporal Clarence R. Van Alen
and Sergeant Clifton Merrimon, of the 372nd, both received the triple decoration of the Croix de Guerre with
palm, the Distinguished Service Cross, and the Medaille
Militaire.

152. Defamation. In spite of this record—perhaps in
some measure because of it—and in the face of his loyal
response to the call of duty, the Negro became in the
course of the war the victim of proscription and propaganda probably without parallel in the history of the
country. No effort seems to have been spared to discredit
him both as a soldier and as a man.

Slanders were deliberately circulated among the
French people, sometimes on high authority; and the
military police shot and killed on the slightest provoca-
tion. At Bourbonne Les Bains the people were told that
they must remain indoors when the Negro soldiers appeared, carry guns, and not under any circumstances to
permit the men to come into their homes.

White women engaged in "Y" work sometimes
showed a disposition to make distinctions in serving
white and Negro soldiers in the canteens; those of the
Red Cross and the Salvation Army were much better
in this respect.

When, on July 14, 1919, Bastille Day, the Allied gen-
erals and their armies had their victory parade in Paris.

no place was found for the Negro; and later a great picture, or series of pictures, that had official co-opera-tion, the "Pantheon de la Guerre," gave representation to all the forces and divisions of the Allied armies except to those of Negroes from the United States.[2]

To all misrepresentation, however, the final reply was that of the Secretary of War, Newton D. Baker, who formally studied the points that had been made, investi-gating them fully, and in his public findings gave a com-plete negation to the charges.

153. The Houston Incident. While the Negro soldier abroad was thus under special pressure, there occurred at home an incident that was singularly depressing.

In August, 1917, just a few weeks after the massacre in East St. Louis, a battalion of the Twenty-fourth In-fantry, stationed at Houston, Texas, encountered the ill will of the town, and between the city police and the Negro military police there was constant friction. At last, when one of the soldiers had been beaten, word was circulated among his comrades that he had been killed, and a number of them set out for revenge. In the riot that followed (August 23) two of the Negroes and seventeen white persons, including five policemen, were killed. As a result of this encounter sixty-three members of the battalion were court-martialed at Fort Sam Hous-ton. Thirteen were hanged on December 11, 1917, five more on September 13; and fifty-one were sentenced to life imprisonment, five being given briefer terms. The

[2] For the whole subject of the life of the Negro soldier, see Charles H. Williams, *Sidelights on Negro Soldiers* (Boston: B. J. Brimmer Co., 1923), an authoritative book giving the result of a first-hand and official investigation.

cases of those imprisoned were later given further review, with some modification of the sentences.

154. Tense Feeling. The sudden close of the war, the conflicting stories that had come from abroad, and the general problem of readjustment all combined to make the year 1919 one of unusual tenseness of feeling.

The old KuKlux began to ride again, and there were acts of violence in various parts of the country. In Tennessee, in less than a year, three Negroes were burned at the stake. In May, 1918, in Brooks County, Georgia, after a harsh employer of labor had beaten a worker and was himself shot a few evenings later, eleven Negroes were lynched, one being a woman who was horribly mutilated; five hundred others felt forced to leave the vicinity. In December of this same year, after the murder of a white dentist who had been interested in one of the young women involved, four young Negroes—two men and two women—were taken from the little jail in Shubuta, Mississippi, and lynched. In the following May, at Milan, Georgia, an aged Negro, Berry Washington, who endeavored to protect two young girls from two drunken white men attempting to invade their home, was killed and his body riddled with bullets. Such occurrences as these ground the iron into the Negro's soul, and as never before he girded himself for resistance.

155. Washington, Chicago, Elaine. The most startling events occurred in two of the greatest cities of the country.

On July 19, 1919, a series of lurid and exaggerated stories in the daily papers of Washington, D. C., resulted in an outbreak that was intended to terrorize the northwest section of the city, in which were some of the best Negro homes. For three days the constituted officers of the law failed to do their duty; then the Negro men assumed their own defense and the rioting ceased.

A week later there burst into flame in Chicago a race war of the greatest fierceness and bitterness. The situation was already tense by reason of the migration from the South; and the stoning and drowning of a Negro boy at a bathing beach but supplied the spark that resulted in the death of twenty Negroes and fourteen white men, in the injuring of scores of other persons, and in the burning of several Negro homes.

In the first week in October there began to come from Elaine, Arkansas, reports of prolonged disorders which found their ultimate origin in the iniquities of the peonage system.

All such events were of course a challenge not only to the Negro but to the nation, and, more than ever, thoughtful and patriotic people felt it necessary to help toward a genuine adjustment.

156. The Negro Press. Meanwhile Negro periodical literature assumed such importance as it never had before, molding opinion with far-reaching effect.

By 1920 there were nearly five hundred publications regularly issued. Of these a little more than eighty were the organs of religious groups, and just about as many were school or college journals; but more than half of the number were weekly papers reviewing current events. Prominent among the monthly magazines were naturally the *Crisis* and *Opportunity*, but also influential for some years was the *Messenger*, a periodical of more radical temper issued in New York.

The foremost of the weeklies then began to go beyond the 100,000 mark in circulation. Among the more prominent were the *Chicago Defender*, the *Pittsburgh Courier*, the *Afro-American* (Baltimore), the *Journal and Guide* (Norfolk), the *Amsterdam News* (New York), the *Savannah Tribune*, the *Philadelphia Tribune*, the *Houston Informer*, the *Call* (Kansas City, Mo.), and the *Black Dispatch* (Oklahoma City, Okla.).

As to the events of the summer of 1919, these papers pointed out that Negroes did not instigate the riots, that those persons who did start them had the assistance of the police, and that investigation after the events failed to tell the true story.

Not all of the journals were equally well printed, and sometimes there was a tendency toward sensationalism; but in general the papers were a unit in their struggle for civic freedom and justice, and each became in its community a medium of racial aspiration.

157. The Widening Problem. In view of the experience of their men in the war in Europe, and of the important part played by the French colonial troops, it is not surprising that the hearts of the Negro people in America quickened with a new sympathy for their brothers the world over.

Already, in 1911, the First Universal Races Congress, meeting in London, had attracted wide attention; and in February, 1919, largely through the effort of Dr. Du Bois, the first of several Pan-African Congresses was held in Paris. Meanwhile the purchase of the Virgin Islands from Denmark had fixed attention upon an interesting colored population at the door of the United States; and, in the second administration of President Wilson, the American occupation of Haiti, resulting in the killing of several persons, led to a new feeling of kinship with the land of Toussaint L'Ouverture.

As never before it was realized that the so-called Negro problem was no longer local in the United States or South Africa, or the West Indies, but international in its scope and outlook.

158. A New Race Consciousness. Out of all the fires of the era came a new consciousness for the Negro, one that he has never since lost.

In some measure this was due to an idea which, after the war, found many adherents in the United States and which fostered operations on a scale that forced recognition. This was the idea of the Provisional Republic of Africa, the Universal Negro Improvement Association, the Black Star line of steamships, and the Negro Factories Corporation, all of which activities, centered in New York, had as their organ the *Negro World,* and as their president and leading spirit Marcus Garvey, who was originally from Jamaica.

The central thought that appealed to hosts of people was that of freedom for the Negro race in every sense of the word. Such freedom, it was declared, transcended the mere demand for certain political and social rights and could finally be realized only under a vast supergovernment guiding the destinies of the race in Africa, the United States, the West Indies, and everywhere else in the world. The related ideas and activities were some-

times termed grandiose, the leaders awakened much opposition, and some of their methods at length brought
them into the courts; nevertheless the general conception
served to give to the young American Negro a quickening that he might not otherwise have had and that even
today continues to influence the group consciousness of
the Negroes in this country.

CHAPTER XV

RECENT HISTORY

159. The New Temper in Negro Life. The dissatisfaction of the American people with some of the later policies of President Wilson, and their weariness of everything pertaining to the war, led them to give a majority of their votes in 1920 to the Republican candidate for the presidency; and the next eight years—those of the administrations of President Harding and Coolidge —became a period of inflated values and surface prosperity such as the country has seldom witnessed before. More and more the political party that began in 1854 with emphasis on simple human rights appeared to have drifted from its moorings and seemed to be a party of privilege and high finance. The reaction came in October, 1929, with a crash in the stock market in New York; and the country entered upon a period of economic stress that sent millions into unemployment and that to many seemed to call for radical measures of relief.

This was the situation with which President Franklin D. Roosevelt was faced when he took office in 1933. The critical years of the era did not fail to affect the temper of the nation. The so-called "post-war generation"—carefree, indifferent, extravagant—was succeeded by a still younger generation, one that longed for a better day but that was without work or tangible hope and assumed toward life a sternly realistic attitude. Young Negro people, like others, came under this new temper, and they too began to question existing institutions and to demand a new economic order. As never before they showed a willingness to suffer for a cause that seemed worth while, and they were not afraid.

160. The Changing Political Front. It was but natural that this new temper should lead among other things to a questioning of the traditional allegiance of the Negro to the Republican party.

As here and there men of the opposing organization showed a disposition to be fair, many Negroes in Northern states were led to vote as Democrats, and in course of time, in several states, they even held the balance of power. This led to a dilemma for the high officials of the party. They naturally valued a vote that might turn an election in a large Northern state; at the same time they had to keep in mind the so-called "Solid South," that had approved disfranchisement and that in general was opposed to a liberal policy either within or without the party. In 1936 there were not less than thirty Negro delegates or alternates at the Democratic National Convention in Philadelphia, and at one of the sessions prayer was offered by the Reverend Marshall L. Shepard, of Philadelphia, who, in addition to being a minister, was also a member of the Pennsylvania state legislature. This was the first time a Negro had so officiated at a Democratic National Convention, and Senator Ellison D. Smith, of South Carolina, attracted some attention by leaving the hall. In 1934 Arthur W. Mitchell, Democrat, was elected to Congress from the first Illinois district, thus displacing the stalwart Oscar DePriest, Republican, who had served for two terms. Mr. Mitchell was reelected in 1936, and again in 1938; and among several members of the race elected to state legislatures in this latter year, distinction attached to Mrs. Crystal Bird Fauset, of Philadelphia, the first woman to be so honored.

As representing the new temper, especially as this affected the younger group of men and women, one might note the organization in Chicago in February, 1936, of the National Negro Congress, which issued its call to all persons, of whatever persuasion, who were willing to fight for economic and social justice for Negroes. Of this organization A. Philip Randolph, of the Brotherhood of Sleeping Car Porters, became president and John P. Davis secretary; and its point of view received strong reinforcement from the platform adopted by The Southern Conference for Human Welfare, organized in Birmingham, Alabama, near the close of November, 1938. To this gathering came not less than twelve hundred Southern men and women, and about three hundred of those enrolled were Negroes. The permanent chairman elected was President Frank P. Graham, of the University of North Carolina; and among the vice-chairmen, representing the Negro people, were John P. Davis and Mrs. Mary McLeod Bethune. In general there was a strong cleavage between the traditional and conservative South and the newer, more forward-looking element. The conference took a stand against segregation laws and all special restrictions on Negro suffrage; it called for the enactment of an antilynching law; and it condemned the brutality at times visited upon Negroes by public officers. At one evening session Mrs. Franklin D. Roosevelt was the principal speaker, and though, at the insistence of the Birmingham police department, there was separation of the races in the seating, the conference next day adopted a resolution providing that no future meeting of the group would be held in any city with a segregation ordinance.

All along, in the period we are considering, members of the Communist party were active; and while their revolutionary program did not appeal to the great host of the Negro people, they did influence the thinking of many young men and women. When in 1932 one of their number, Angelo Herndon, of Cincinnati, was arrested in Atlanta, Georgia, on a charge of circulating incendiary literature, and the next year was sentenced to imprisonment for not less than eighteen years or more than twenty, they fought the decision from one court to another until in April, 1937, the United States Supreme Court ruled, by a five to four decision, that the sentence imposed under an old Georgia statute was unconstitutional.

161. The Negro and the "New Deal." In his endeavor to meet the crisis that he found facing the country, especially the widespread unemployment, President Roosevelt entered upon a vast program of social amelioration commonly known as the "New Deal." This led to the organization of a number of new Federal bureaus. At the basis of the whole structure was the National Industrial Recovery Act, which was approved in June, 1933, and designed "to encourage national industrial recovery, to foster fair competition, and to provide for the construction of certain useful public works, and for other purposes." The NRA (National Recovery Administration), which the act fostered, was fiercely assailed by many business men as hampering production and exerting undue bureaucratic influence; and the act itself was declared unconstitutional by the Supreme Court in May, 1935. Other agencies fared somewhat better. The FERA (Federal Emergency Relief Administration) provided for the co-operation of the Federal government with the different states in the relief of the suffering caused by unemployment and drought. The WPA (Works Progress Administration) was designed to remove from the relief rolls for work on special projects the maximum number of people in the shortest time possible. The CCC (Civilian Conservation Corps) was intended both to provide employment for able-bodied young men who were out of work and to restore the depleted natural resources of the United States, or otherwise advance an orderly program of public works. The NYA (National Youth Administration) was organized as a part of the effort of the WPA, the major objectives being to find employment in private industry for young people without work, to give to many of them assignments on projects suited to their ability, to provide vocational guidance for those without specific training, and to extend part-time employment to needy high-school, college, and graduate students between sixteen and twenty-five years of age. Even these relief agencies were not accepted without strong criticism, many earnest persons feeling that they not only led to undue competition with private business but also undermined self-reliance by encouraging dependence on the Government, while at the other extreme were those radicals who felt that the whole program was merely palliative and should go much farther than it did.

As to the relation of the Negro to the new agencies, the policy of the administration was clearly stated by President Roosevelt in a speech at the dedication of the new Chemistry Building at Howard University in October, 1936, in the words, "There must be no forgotten men and no forgotten races." As among those who suffered most from poverty and lack of employment, the Negro people were naturally prominent among those dependent on direct relief; but they also found a place in such other agencies as have been mentioned. Representative men and women of the race were also placed in important administrative posts; thus Lieutenant Lawrence A. Oxley became chief of the Division of Negro Labor in the Department of Labor; Dr. Robert G. Weaver became assistant to the administrator of the United States Housing Authority; and Mrs. Mary McLeod Bethune, president of Bethune-Cookman College, became director of the Division of Negro Affairs in the National Youth Administration.

162. CCC and NYA. Two agencies, not far apart in aim, may serve to show the scope of the efforts of the new organizations in their relation to the Negro.

By January, 1938, after five years of activity, the CCC had organized 152 camps for young Negro men, and in these 30,446 individuals had been enrolled. In order to promote the efficiency of these future citizens, the camps endeavored not only to give training in special projects,

but also to remove early defects in education, to emphasize cultural values, and in general to assist those enrolled
to use their leisure time to advantage. More than 53 per
cent of the young men enrolled were found to be on the
elementary-school level, but not less than 87 per cent of
the total number voluntarily embraced the opportunity
afforded for literary improvement. As the educational
program for each camp had to be worked out independently, the adviser in the field had to exert his initiative; but, as he was regularly the only Negro member of
the supervisory personnel, he also had an unusual opportunity in the general life of the camp. In course of time
two thirds of the camps had papers edited and published
by the men enrolled.

In the NYA a report of April 2, 1938, said that 36,000
Negro students were earning wages totalling approxi-
mately $200,000 a month; that $70,000 per annum had
been set aside for a Graduate Fund; that 18,000 Negro
youth were earning over $250,000 a month erecting
various structures, making playgrounds and roadside
parks, or doing clerical or research work; and that 1,200
young men and women, out of school and unemployed,
were enrolled in centers near educational institutions for
instruction in farming technique and home management.
However, two men who studied the organization con-
cluded that even in the NYA Negro youth were not
receiving their just share of Federal funds, that in fact
they had received only "about one half of the administration and supervision provided in the states, about
two thirds of the school and work opportunities, and

less than one sixteenth of the guidance and placement services required," plainly less than his due.[1]

163. The Problem of Crime.   Throughout the years we are considering, attention continued to be fixed upon the grave problem of crime; and this has connection with some other subjects we are yet to discuss.

About no phase of the life of the Negro in America is it more difficult to get reliable statistics. Figures are often given on the basis of the number of arrests; but, if one remembers that when a Negro is accused of a crime, there is often a "round-up," meaning that several persons are held for investigation when only one may be guilty, these figures prove to be unreliable. It is known too that white men have often disguised themselves as black men before committing offenses, and that policemen are often brutal in their treatment of Negroes. One might also note the background of the life of most men accused—the crowded conditions in many slums and tenements and the high proportion of unemployment. All these things must be considered.

Yet, when all possible factors have been weighed, crime remains the most deplorable aspect of the life of the Negro in America. In larceny, assault, and burglary the percentage is altogether too high.

164. The Scottsboro Case.   It was the fact that it touched upon one phase of this large subject of crime that gave

---

[1] See Walter G. Daniel and Carroll L. Miller, "The Participation of the Negro in the National Youth Administration Program," *Journal of Negro Education*, VII (July, 1938); also Howard W. Oxley, "The Civilian Conservation Corps and the Education of the Negro." *Journal of Negro Education*, VII (July, 1938).

significance to one of the most far-reaching cases that have ever affected the Negro in American courts.

On March 25, 1931, nine Negro boys and young men, ranging in age from thirteen to twenty years, were arrested at Paint Rock, Alabama, and accused of attacking two young white women on a freight train. It appeared that the young women were dressed in overalls and "beating" their way from Chattanooga, Tennessee, to Huntsville, Alabama. Within a week all of the youths were indicted by the grand jury of Jackson County on a charge of rape. On April 6, in the trial at Scottsboro, two of the young men were given the death sentence, and within the next three days other convictions followed, though that of the youngest boy was later set aside on the ground that he was a juvenile.

Then began a struggle, the details of which would fill a large book, in which members of the Communist party were prominent among those who sprang to the defense of the young men, and which at the close of 1938 was still before the American public. The fundamental assumption attacked was the one common in the South that the testimony of a white woman against a Negro was to be accepted whether the facts supported the testimony or not. Moreover, it was brought out that Negroes were regularly denied service on juries throughout the South. On March 25, 1932, the Alabama Supreme Court affirmed the sentences imposed by the circuit court, but in the following November the United States Supreme Court set these aside on the ground that the Negroes had not had the benefit of adequate counsel. In March, 1933, a change of venue was granted from Scottsboro in

Jackson County to Decatur in Morgan County, and the defense now made much of the fact that no Negroes were on the jury rolls. At this juncture one of the young women repudiated her earlier account of the attacks, charging that her companion had made up the story. All the same, on April 9, Heywood Patterson, who had now become prominent among the young men accused, was sentenced to death. On June 22 Judge James E. Horton set aside the sentence, holding that the evidence was insufficient, and ordered a new trial. On December 1 judgment was passed on Patterson for the third time, and in June, 1934, his and the other sentences were confirmed by the Alabama Supreme Court. On April 1, 1935, the United State Supreme Court held that the constitutional rights of the defendants had been violated in that Negroes had been excluded from jury service; but in the following January Patterson was again convicted, though this time sentence was for seventy-five years. In July, 1937, four of the young men were set free, but the others still remained in prison under varying terms.

Important in connection with the Scottsboro Case was an opinion handed down by Chief Justice Hughes, of the United States Supreme Court, in April, 1938, to the effect that the systematic and arbitrary exclusion of Negroes from jury lists in Kentucky was sufficient reason for ordering a new trial of a Negro convicted of murder. The opinion said that the exclusion of Negroes from the jury lists solely because of their race and color constituted a denial of the equal protection of the laws guaranteed by the Fourteenth Amendment to the Federal Constitution; and Kentucky was thus warned to end a condition that had endured in that state and in several other states for more than fifty years.

165. The Church in the Changing Order. While these important events affecting the Negro were taking place, just what was the situation or advance in such large fields of effort as those of religion, education, and industry?

As to the first of these it must be said that the situation left much to be desired. The realistic temper of the age did not make for a vital personal religion, and even earnest worshippers felt that the church as an institution could be more active in responding to the needs of the age. Meanwhile, especially in the larger centers, various new cults flourished, some with sensational modes of worship; and in more than one there was a tendency toward paganism.

In 1938 there were in round terms 3,250,000 Negro members in the Baptist denomination, 650,000 in the African Methodist Episcopal, 500,000 in the African Methodist Episcopal Zion, 350,000 in the Methodist Episcopal, and 250,000 in the Colored Methodist Episcopal. There were also 55,000 Episcopalians, 40,000 Presbyterians, 20,000 Congregationalists, and 250,000 Roman Catholics. It thus appears that the Baptists are greatly in the majority, that in fact they form hardly less than 60 per cent of the entire church membership. In other words we may say that six out of every ten Negroes who belong to the church are Baptists, and that nine out of every ten are either Baptists or Methodists. In recent years the National Baptist Convention has greatly improved in organization, especially in the conduct of its foreign mission work.

In the spring of 1936 a special question affecting the Negro arose in the Methodist Episcopal Church. This organization was moving toward reunion with the Methodist Episcopal Church, South, and it had been proposed that Negro communicants be placed in a separate conference. The great majority of responsible Negroes opposed the plan, but the General Conference voted for segregation. To many who had hoped for the practical application of Christian principles, this seemed like a backward step. Hardly less significant was a new policy of segregation adopted by the Christian Science Church, with headquarters in Boston. However, in another religious group, the Episcopalian, that formerly had been most conservative, a notable step forward was taken at a conference in Chicago in the late autumn of 1938. A resolution that was adopted favored the opening of all the colleges and seminaries operated by the Episcopal Church to Negro aspirants for the priesthood, and in general it was urged that all the agencies and auxiliaries of the church be made available to Negroes as well as to other groups.

While the formally organized religious bodies sometimes seemed to make little progress in securing better relations between the races and in thus exhibiting a truly Christian spirit, various groups of young people showed a disposition to act independently. Representative was the recently organized United Christian Youth Movement of America, with headquarters in Chicago. The Movement is interdenominational, and it aims to cut across all barriers of race or creed, uniting all groups of young people in a fellowship vitally Christian. It is worthy of note that the first president was a young man of Negro descent, Martin Harvey, a graduate of New York University.

166. Reorganization in Education. A Significant Court Decision. In the education of the Negro the ten years between 1928 and 1938 witnessed remarkable readjustment.

The Northern missionary agencies that had led in higher training found it more and more necessary to curtail or concentrate their efforts, and some of the great philanthropic boards that had helped most vitally began to close their work.

The burden was thus thrown where it rightly belonged, upon the states; and enlightened officials, such as those in North Carolina (among them N. C. Newbold), helped notably with their vision and public spirit. In several of the land-grant colleges there was distinct advance, and modern high-school buildings superseded the inadequate structures of an earlier day. The plant at Howard was practically rebuilt, the most impressive of several new buildings being the Founders Library, erected at a cost of $1,106,000; and university centers also began to develop in Atlanta, Nashville, and New Orleans. Hampton and Tuskegee, that had swung far from their old moorings toward the aims of the liberal arts colleges, now deemed it advisable to re-examine themselves; and at Tuskegee especially, under a new president, F. D. Patterson, there was a new response to the demands of practical life.

Suddenly, in December, 1938, there was handed down from the Supreme Court of the United States a decision that seemed destined to have far-reaching effect on the whole fabric of education in the South. For some years the point had been made here and there that a Southern state could not be justified in maintaining a university offering graduate instruction in such fields as medicine and law and in refusing at the same time to admit a Negro interested in those fields. This situation some states met by giving advanced Negro students scholarships to study elsewhere, though Maryland admitted a Negro to the Law School of the state university. The case before the Supreme Court was that of Lloyd L. Gaines, of St. Louis, in his relation to the Law School of the University of Missouri; and Chief Justice Hughes in 1938 delivered the majority opinion (6 to 2) that Missouri, in compelling colored law students to attend institutions outside the state, had violated the provisions of the Federal Constitution, that "a privilege has been created for white law students which is denied to Negroes by reason of their race," and that "the provision for the payment of tuition fees in another State does not remove the discrimination." [2] It thus appeared that henceforth it would be necessary for a Southern state to follow the lead of the University of Maryland and admit a Negro student, or go to the vast expense of providing for separate university training. In addition the decision was not least effective in calling attention to the general inequality in education in the South.

[2] "Missouri Ex Rel. Gaines v. Canada," *Official Reports of the Supreme Court*, Vol. 305 U. S., No. 2, 338.

167. Labor Organization. The Brotherhood of Sleeping Car Porters. The years that we are now considering also saw the Negro assuming a new place in the forces of organized labor in the United States.

From the first there had been discerning men in the labor movement who felt that the interest of their cause demanded that they rise above distinctions of race or class; and when the American Federation of Labor was organized in 1884, it began by opposing any discrimination. Twenty years later, however, there developed a change of policy. The Negro was more and more proscribed, and successive conventions of the Federation evaded the issue.

This was still the situation in 1936, in which year a new and more radical organization, the CIO (Committee for Industrial Organization), was challenging the Federation all along the line. To the CIO it seemed that the AFL was not sufficiently aggressive and that it was even unduly dominated by capitalism. Against the CIO itself the points were made that its temper was largely that of Communism and that some of its methods, such as that of the "sit-down strike," which entailed a seizure of property, could find no legal justification. At any rate, for the time being it was the CIO that was the more active in the cause of the Negro.

Representative of the efforts of the CIO was the organization of the Tobacco Stemmers' and Laborers' Industrial Union in and near Richmond, Virginia, in 1937. Within eighteen months the workers in the factories had won an eight-hour day where formerly they had labored from nine to twelve or even more hours, and their purchasing power had been increased by hundreds of thousands of dollars.[3] This result was in challenging contrast to the old idea of the Negro worker, that he fared better with plant managers and was generally better off if he did not join a union.

As to the question, is the Negro being influenced by the CIO? an investigator, T. Arnold Hill, said, "A fair answer is that he is joining the steel workers' organizations when the number of Negroes in an industry being organized is sufficiently large to warrant special efforts on the part of the labor union to get Negroes to join." [4] However, it appears in the main "that the Negro is not yet labor conscious; that he is not yet ready to join either the A. F. of L. or the CIO or any other union for fear that the slight gain he has made in industry will be lost. He has not yet sensed the possibility of exclusion if he fails to join a labor union which subsequently becomes the bargaining union group." [5]

Important in the whole relation of the Negro to collective bargaining was the organization in New York City in August, 1925, of the Brotherhood of Sleeping Car Porters, of which A. Philip Randolph became president. The object was to reduce the hours of work required and to secure wages commensurate with health, comfort, and the enjoyment of higher cultural standards.

[3] See Augusta V. Jackson, "A New Deal for Tobacco Workers," the *Crisis*, October, 1938.

[4] T. Arnold Hill, "The Negro and the CIO," *Opportunity*, XV (August, 1937), 243, 244.

[5] A. Philip Randolph, "Pullman Porters Win," *Opportunity*, October, 1937, 299-300; and G. James Fleming, "Pullman Porters Win Pot of Gold," the *Crisis*, XLIV (November, 1937), 332-333, 338.

Formerly the wage of a porter was $67.50 a month, with no security on the job, and his work-month of 300 to 400 hours required him to travel an average of 11,000 miles. In the course of its effort the Brotherhood had to struggle against coercion and intimidation on the part of the Pullman management, against the admonition of many Negro leaders, and even against opposition from some men within the ranks; but at length, on August 25, 1937, exactly twelve years from the date of its birth, it concluded with the Pullman Company an agreement that secured for the men an increase of $12 a month (this aggregating $1,250,000 a year) and a 240-hour work-month. The Brotherhood of Sleeping Car Porters is affiliated with the American Federation of Labor as an international union, and it is the first such union organized and controlled by Negroes. However, some men of other races—Chinese, Filipinos, Mexicans—are also members, and white barbers on Pullman cars have also applied for membership and have been accepted.

CHAPTER XVI

SOCIAL AND ECONOMIC PROGRESS

168. General Advance. Within the years since emancipation, the Negro race has not only advanced in home-life, organization, and art, but in almost every field of endeavor has produced individuals whose achievements challenge consideration by the highest standards of American culture. Along with general progress has gone increasing racial consciousness.

In the professions and special occupations one finds architects, chemists, metallurgists, designers, and other skilled workers in ever-increasing number; and more and more these people have made themselves a necessary element in the civilization of which they are a part.

Nearly a thousand men are now engaged in journalism; five or six thousand more are in printing or engraving; and through such magazines as the *Crisis* and *Opportunity*, and such weekly papers as the *Chicago Defender*, the *Pittsburgh Courier*, the *Afro-American* (Baltimore), and the *Journal and Guide* (Norfolk), the aspiration of the race finds expression, while the quarterly *Journal of Negro History* and *Journal of Negro Education* are representative of endeavor in the higher fields of scholarship.

169. Home Life and Health. In no way perhaps has the general advance been better shown than in the improved conditions of home life; yet there is no phase of the life of the Negro that must still give more concern.

By the census of 1930 very nearly one fourth of the total of 2,803,756 Negro homes were reported as owned; and the percentage was considerably higher in urban than in rural areas. In the North, where the Negro population is less stable than in the South, greater use is made of temporary abodes; thus in a crowded center like New York City, lodgers hardly ever constitute less than a third of the population. Different places show the greatest possible disparity; in some cities to which a few years ago there was much migration, the percentage of owned homes is not more than 4 or 5 per cent, while in exceptionally favored communities it has been as high as 80 per cent.

The movement to the cities has led to much crowding in tenements and slum areas, and thus we are forced to consider the important subject of mortality. The figures are depressing. In 1933 the death rate of Negroes was higher than the birth rate in eleven states, and in general the death rate was considerably higher than that for the white people. In the city of Washington, in November, 1938, a medical official affirmed that though the Negro people formed but 25 per cent of the total population, they made up 63 per cent of those who died of tuberculosis. However, with greater enlightenment and the increasing care given by hospitals, there is steady improvement; thus, while in 1911 the rate in tuberculosis was 405.3 for each 100,000 Negroes, by 1933 the figure had been reduced to 104.3. Vital is the point that, as the number of owned homes in a given area increases, the mortality figures also decrease.

Strong incentive to more wholesome living was given in the administrations of President Franklin D. Roosevelt by vast home-building projects in a number of the larger cities; and while it is true that homes designed to relieve congestion in slum areas were actually often occupied by people in the middle class of wage-earners, the general effect was both far-reaching and beneficent.

170. Business and Industry. In the wider field of business the Negro is also developing his enterprises. In all there are today in the United States about 75,000 business concerns operated by Negroes. Most numerous still are restaurants, lunchrooms, and grocery stores, though within recent years occupations centered around garages, filling stations, and automobile repair shops have shown notable advance. In the previous chapter we considered the relation of the Negro to the labor movement, and the organization of such a union as the Brotherhood of Sleeping Car Porters, indicative of his importance in the railroad industry. His most profitable field of employment is still that of contracting in building work, with printing and publishing next in importance. By reason of the amount of capital invested, however, life insurance is the most important field of business in which members of the colored race are now engaged. In 1936 there were 44 Negro companies, and of these 28 were members of the National Negro Insurance Association. These companies had in force $288,963,070 worth of insurance on 1,643,125 policies. Outstanding is the North Carolina Mutual Life Insurance Company, with headquarters in

Durham. Prominent in their field, that of the manufacture of toilet preparations, are the Madam C. J. Walker Manufacturing Company, with headquarters in Indianapolis, and Poro College in St. Louis, founded by Mrs. A. M. Malone.

In order to see the great change that has taken place within the last fifty years, one may note that in 1890 55.8 per cent of the Negro people at work were engaged in agriculture, 31 per cent in domestic or personal service, and only 13 per cent in all other occupations, but that in 1930 34.7 per cent, or more than one third, were in fields of labor other than farming or domestic service.

Even yet, however, if we take into account farming, the building trades, and saw and planing mills, and consider also those men engaged as railway firemen and porters, draymen, teamsters, and coal-mine operatives, we shall find that not less than 70 per cent are engaged in such work as represents the very foundation of American industry.

An important question affecting business and industry was constantly at issue throughout the recent Roosevelt administrations. When legislation looked toward raising the wages of workers in the lowest economic group, again and again it was insisted in some quarters that there would have to be a "differential" for the South. This meant that many industries in the South would be excused from the general provisions of such a proposed enactment as the Wage and Hour Law, so that there would be no radical change in the lot of Negro and poor white laborers. As to this the Raleigh *News and Observer* well said: "The wage differential operates to withhold from the South the same measure of buying power and recovery which it provides for other sections. . . . It operates not only against a Negro man or woman working in a laundry, but directly against every Southern wage earner, every Southern merchant, every Southern lawyer or doctor."

171. Invention. Reference has already been made to the original inventive work of Benjamin Banneker.

As to devices formally registered in the United States Patent Office, it is difficult to gave an exact figure for those by Negroes, as race does not figure in registration. However, 3,000 would be a conservative estimate.[1] As we have seen, the honor of receiving the first patent granted to any man in the race belongs to Henry Blair, of Maryland, who in 1834 took out a patent for a corn harvester.

At about the close of the last century Granville T. Woods surpassed every other inventor of his race in the number and variety of his devices. His record began in 1884 in Cincinnati, Ohio, where he then resided, and continued without interruption until his death in New York in 1910. Among his inventions were various improvements in telegraphy, and many of his patents were assigned to such companies as the General Electric, of New York, and the American Bell Telephone, of Boston.

[1] Henry E. Baker, for years an employee in the United States Patent Office, issued through the Crisis Publishing Company a pamphlet, *The Colored Inventor*, and contributed "The Negro in the Field of Invention," to the *Journal of Negro History* for *January*, 1917. He gave the figure as about 1,000, but there has been rapid advance within recent years.

Elijah McCoy, who began his work in 1872, was granted fifty-seven patents, these relating chiefly to lubricating appliances for engines. He was a pioneer in the art of steadily supplying oil to machinery from a cup, so that it would not be necessary to stop a machine in order to oil it. His inventions were long in use on various railroads and the steamships of the Great Lakes.

Jan E. Matzeliger, born in Dutch Guiana in 1852, came to the United States as a young man and served as cobbler's apprentice first in Philadelphia, Pennsylvania, then in Lynn, Massachusetts. The hardships to which he was subjected undermined his health, and he died in 1889 in his thirty-seventh year, but not before he had invented a machine for attaching soles to shoes, the first appliance of its kind capable of performing all the steps required to hold a shoe on its last, grip and pull the leather down around the heel, guide and drive the nails into place, and then discharge the completed shoe from the machine. The patent for this invention was bought by the United Shoe Machinery Company, of Boston, and Matzeliger's invention thus became the basis of a great enterprise that represents the consolidation of forty subsidiary enterprises and gives employment to tens of thousands of people.

Notable for the variety of their inventions were also J. H. Dickinson and his son, S. L. Dickinson, both of New Jersey, who were granted numerous patents for their appliances, mainly in the line of devices connected with the operation of the player piano. W. B. Purvis, of Philadelphia, took out more than a dozen patents having to do with machinery for the making of paper bags; and

Benjamin O. Jackson, of Massachusetts, has been granted nearly as many for inventions that include a heating apparatus, a gas burner, and a trolley-wheel controller.

Among the numerous inventions of very recent years we may note, as representative, the following: a burglar trap, by H. Jackson, of Harrisburg, Pennsylvania, which so works as to imprison a bandit in a bullet-proof cage; a pecan thrasher, by E. D. McBryer, of Boley, Oklahoma; an automobile air pump, by A. B. Williamson, of Lula, Mississippi; various devices by different men for the improvement of aeroplanes; and the highly promising work of Claude Harvard, a young employee of the Ford Motor Company in Detroit, who assisted H. A. Chubbuck of the firm in the building of a piston-pin testing machine and demonstrated this at the Century of Progress Exposition in Chicago.[2]

172. Professions and Public Life. In the learned professions of ministry, law, and medicine, the Negro has made rapid progress within recent decades. In fact, if to these be added teaching and, for the more recent years, business, we shall have the fields upon which his race has depended in the main for its leadership.

These professions are frequently thought to be crowded; but in law, medicine, and dentistry the ratio to the Negro population is still far below that in these fields to the general population. The total number of Negroes in the professions is now about 120,000. This figure includes 60,000 teachers, 26,000 ministers, 4,000

[2] For a more extended list of inventions by Negroes within recent years see the *Negro Year Book* (ed. Monroe N. Work), 1937-1938, pp. 12-13.

physicians, 1,800 dentists, 1,500 lawyers, 12,000 musicians, and an increasing number of actors, trained nurses, and social workers.

Within the last three decades women have made noteworthy advance in all the arts and professions, with the exception of the ministry.[3] In individual cases they are outstanding, and numerically in music and the other arts the ratio of men to women is just about 3 to 2.

In general, in spite of the opportunities offered by schools and colleges, the ministry has not advanced in training as rapidly as the other professions. In the state of North Carolina it was found in 1930 that in the large Baptist and Methodist denominations not less than 70 per cent of the ministers had not gone in academic training beyond the eighth grade. While uneducated men have often had great spiritual insight and power, and while today there are well-trained men in all the denominations, it is obvious that the proper preparation of the minister is still one of the pressing problems facing the Negro people.

To the lawyers has fallen much of the leadership in public affairs. Among those men who have been prominent since 1900 one might note Judson W. Lyons, William T. Vernon, and J. C. Napier as registers of the Treasury of the United States; Charles W. Anderson as collector of internal revenue for the Second District of New York; William H. Lewis as assistant attorney general of the United States; and Arthur H. Mitchell

[3] See Benjamin Brawley, *Negro Builders and Heroes* (Chapel Hill· The University of North Carolina Press, 1936), pp. 260-288.

(Democrat), elected to Congress from the First District in Illinois in 1934, and elected for a third term in 1938.

173. Medicine. The history of the Negro physician is of more than usual interest and importance.

We have already remarked the pioneer work of James Derham early in the last century and the training of a number of young men by the American Colonization Society. After the Civil War, medical departments were established in a number of institutions; but, by reason of the expense of highly specialized and technical study, most of these are no longer in existence. Only the School of Medicine at Howard University and the Meharry Medical College in Nashville now survive, and these institutions are steadily broadening the scope of their activities.

In the years just after the Civil War, two physicians in the District of Columbia were especially prominent. One of these, A. T. Augusta, studied medicine at the University of Toronto and became the first Negro to hold a position as surgeon in the United States Army. Charles B. Purvis, a graduate of the Medical College at Western Reserve University in Cleveland, also became a surgeon in the Army and was for a long period connected with the Freedmen's Hospital in Washington. He was outstanding in the early development of the School of Medicine at Howard.

Later in the century, also, two Negro doctors won signal recognition. Daniel Hale Williams, who received the degree of Doctor of Medicine at Northwestern University in 1883, was for four years a member of the Illinois State Board of Health. He was active in the founding of Provident Hospital in Chicago; in 1893 he became famous by reason of a successful operation on the human heart; and for five years thereafter he was surgeon-in-chief at the Freedmen's Hospital in Washington, D. C. Solomon C. Fuller, who received the degree of Doctor of Medicine at Boston University in 1897, later served for years as professor of neurology at that institution.

Several younger men are just now rising to the height of their careers. William A. Hinton (M.D., Harvard) has been serving for some years as chief of the Wassermann Laboratory of the Massachusetts Department of Public Health and as instructor in Bacteriology in the Harvard Medical School. Julian H. Lewis (M.D., Ph.D., Chicago) is associate professor of pathology at the University of Chicago and pathologist at Provident Hospital. Louis T. Wright (M.D., Harvard) has specialized more and more in injuries to the head, and is now a police surgeon in the city of New York. Several men on the staff at Howard are now going steadily forward in research. Among them are Hildrus A. Poindexter (M.D., Harvard; Ph.D., Columbia), head of the department of Bacteriology and Preventive Medicine, and Arnold H. Maloney (M.D., Indiana; Ph.D., Wisconsin), professor of Pharmacology.

174. Scholarship and Special Distinction. It is not only in the field of medicine that investigators are now engaged in original work; there are those in chemistry, history, and social science who are not less active.

More and more these earnest students conduct their pursuits in accord with regular academic standards, so

feated in the twelfth round by the German, Max Schmel-
ing; but two years later, in a return engagement, he won
over his opponent in the very first round.

In professional baseball, the Negro was proscribed,
but about 1904 William C. Matthews, of Harvard, was
prominent as a player for two or three years.

In football, several men have won places on the foremost college teams in the country. William H. Lewis
became famous as a center at Harvard in the early 90's;
and Matthew W. Bullock, an end, was prominent at
Dartmouth a decade later. Robert Marshall, of the University of Minnesota, won "All-American" distinction
in 1905; and so did Fritz Pollard, of Brown, in 1916, and
Paul Robeson, of Rutgers, in 1918. In 1935 Ozie Sim-
mons, of the University of Iowa, a halfback, attracted
attention by his elusive running; and the next year
Homer Harris, also of Iowa, was elected captain of the
team. In 1938, in a season that produced many highly
capable players, Jerome (Brud) Holland, an end at Cor-
nell, for the second successive year won All-American
honors.

Young Negro athletes of prominence in various other
sports have now become so numerous that only a few of
the foremost can be mentioned, notably those representing the United States in the Olympic games. At about
the turn of the century, Major Taylor was a champion
bicycle rider. A year or two later John B. Taylor, of the
University of Pennsylvania, became the first man of his
race to break intercollegiate records in running, and in
1908 he became the first Negro to represent America in
the Olympic games. At the Olympic games in Paris in

1924, Edwin O. Gourdin, of Harvard, DeHart Hubbard, of Michigan, and R. Earl Johnson, of the Thompson Steel Works in Pittsburgh, were on the team that represented the United States; and Hubbard, in spite of a strained tendon, excelled in the running broad jump, thus becoming the first Negro to win an Olympic championship. The Negro race was not prominently represented in the 1928 games, but in 1932 four young men withstood the trials and won places on the American team—Eddie Tolan, formerly of the University of Michigan, Ralph Metcalfe, from Marquette, Edward L. Gordon, of the University of Iowa, and Cornelius C. Johnson, of the Los Angeles High School. In the 100-meter race Tolan and Metcalfe were so close at the finish that the judges had to see the moving pictures before they finally decided in favor of Tolan. This same runner in the 200-meter event did the best work of his career, winning in 21.2 seconds for a new Olympic and a new world mark. The record was continued and even surpassed at the eleventh Olympiad in Berlin in August, 1936. Negro athletes were the sensation of the meet, and they rapidly captured first places to bring victory to the United States. Jesse Owens, of Cleveland and Ohio State University, won the 100-meter and the 200-meter races; Archie Williams, of California, the 400-meter; and John Woodruff, of the University of Pittsburgh, the 800-meter race. In addition, Cornelius Johnson, of California, broke the record in the high jump, Owens won the broad jump, and Owens and Metcalfe were respectively the first and second runners on the victorious relay team. The outstanding performer of the Olympiad was Owens, who by his individual achievements and work in the relay won four gold medals, with souvenir oaktrees. Five times he surpassed the Olympic broad-jump record, and his feat in breaking that for 200 meters, in the face of a cold wind and on a rain-soaked track, was especially astonishing to the spectators. At the close of the year, in a poll conducted by writers for the Associated Press, he was easily given place as the foremost American athlete in 1936.

In connection with the general subject of sport, significance attaches to an unusual incident in the closing days of July, 1938. Just before a baseball game in Chicago in which the New York team of the American League participated, one of the players on the team, Alvin Powell, was being interviewed over the radio. On being asked what he did when he was not playing ball, he replied jocularly to the effect that he was a policeman and spent his time cracking Negroes over the head; and instead of the word "Negroes" he used an epithet regarded by the race as a whole as highly offensive. Immediately the broadcasting station and the baseball offices were deluged with protests. The player was suspended for ten days by Commissioner K. M. Landis, and even after the expiration of that period the management did not deem it advisable for him to appear on the field in several of the cities of the North.

CHAPTER XVII

LITERATURE AND ART

176. Folklore and Folk Music. In the life and history of the Negro people in America there has developed a notable tradition of customs, superstitions, and tales. Of the Negro literary leaders who were prominent before the Civil War, Frederick Douglass and William Wells Brown were among the first to realize the significance of this material; but it remained for Charles W. Chesnutt, thirty years later, to give it lasting literary form. Other American writers, among them George W. Cable and Thomas Nelson Page, have also found it of service; and its chief literary monument so far has been in the tales of Uncle Remus told by Joel Chandler Harris.

Important as is the folklore, however, the folk music is still more so. This has been both secular and religious. Representative of the secular songs at their best are those that have gathered about the name of John Henry, who had a contest in steel-driving against a steam drill, in which he was victor at the cost of his life. The ballads seem to have been based on an incident that occurred on the C. & O. Railroad in West Virginia about 1871. The religious melodies range all the way from those exhibiting the fundamental character of native African music to those showing a blending with more sophisticated American song. Some were adaptations of Baptist or

Methodist hymns. Those that are most original reflect the sorrow of a struggling people in a dark day. Typical are "My Lord, what a mornin' " and "I'm rollin' through an unfriendly world"; but sometimes the note of triumph sounds with tremendous force, as in "Oh, give way, Jordan." No one is yet able to say how many of these melodies are in existence, for, though there have been many collections, no one is definitive. Unlike the English and Scottish popular ballads, they depend for their merit far more upon their tunes than upon their words. They are also more affected by nature than the ballads. A meteoric shower, a thunderstorm, or the dampness of a furrow was sufficient to give birth to a hymn, and there was free use of figures of speech. As in the ballads, the sentiment of the individual becomes universal; and there is a strong tendency toward repetition. The time structure has sometimes astonished musicians by its accuracy, but in recent years there has been much debasement. The distinction between "ragtime," "jazz," and "swing," on the one hand, and the pure "spirituals," on the other, cannot be too much insisted upon; and more and more the current debasement of Negro rhythms should be discouraged in favor of contribution to the body of true Negro melodies, which represent one of the finest collections of folk music in the world.

177. Crummell, Williams, Whitman and Others. We have seen in previous chapters that, even in the era of the Revolution, Jupiter Hammon and Phillis Wheatley made a beginning in literary achievement, and that, in the decade before the Civil War, William Wells Brown and James M. Whitfield were among those who en-

deavored to carry forward the light. In the years between 1865 and 1890, the men best known for their literary productions were Alexander Crummell, minister and essayist; George W. Williams, the historian; and Albery A. Whitman, a poet. Well known also were such public speakers as Douglass, Robert B. Elliott, and John M. Langston, and popular throughout the period on the lecture platform was Frances E. W. Harper, who often recited her rhythmical verse with telling effect.

Crummell, who received his college degree at Cambridge in England, gave twenty years of his life to Africa and later served as rector of St. Luke's Episcopal Church in Washington. Tall, and noble of bearing, he was distinguished as a lecturer. He brought his addresses and papers together in three collections, *The Future of Africa* (1862), *The Greatness of Christ, and Other Sermons* (1882), and *Africa and America* (1891).

Williams, working often against great privation, blazed a new path, far surpassing any previous effort in the field with his *History of the Negro Race in America from 1619 to 1880*, issued in two large volumes in 1883 by G. P. Putnam's Sons. Five years later appeared *A History of the Negro Troops in the War of the Rebellion*.

Whitman, a minister in the African Methodist Episcopal Church, had the sensitiveness, the imagination, and the fluency of the genuine poet, though his work might have been helped by more discipline. Best known of his publications is *Twasinta's Seminoles, or The Rape of Florida* (1884), an interesting although not altogether successful effort in the Spenserian stanza.

178. Charles W. Chesnutt. Charles Waddell Chesnutt (1858-1932) won such a place in literature as had not previously been attained by any man identified with the Negro people.

Born in Cleveland, Ohio, at the age of sixteen he began to teach in the public schools of North Carolina, from which state his parents had gone, and when twenty-three became principal of the State Normal School in Fayetteville. In 1883 he left the South, engaging for a short while in newspaper work in New York City, but going soon to Cleveland, where he worked as a stenographer and was admitted to the bar.

In 1887 he began in *The Atlantic Monthly* a series of stories based on the superstitions of the Negroes living near the coast in North Carolina. These he later brought together in a volume entitled *The Conjure Woman* (1899). This was soon followed by *The Wife of his Youth, and Other Stories of the Color Line* (1899), in which the title piece is a work of art superb in its intensity. Both of these collections and the first two of the author's novels were published by the Houghton Mifflin Company of Boston. The first novel, *The House behind the Cedars* (1900), treats in the story of the heroine, Rena Walden, some of the most searching questions raised by the color line. *The Marrow of Tradition* (1901), based on the Wilmington riots of 1898, touches upon practically every phase of the race problem. *The Colonel's Dream* (1905) gives the experience of one who was originally from the South and who had achieved success in New York. Colonel Henry French, back on a visit, has a vision of "a regenerated South, filled with thriving industries, and thronged with a prosperous and happy people"; but when he opposed the injustice visited upon the Negro in court and the employment of white children in the mills, he encounters strong resistance and finally goes back to New York defeated. Chesnutt also wrote a compact life of Frederick Douglass in the series of Beacon Biographies of Eminent Americans. He used simple, clear English, worked with a sure sense of art, and must also be given the credit that belongs to a pioneer.

179. **Paul Laurence Dunbar.** The story of Paul Laurence Dunbar (1872-1906) is one of a grinding struggle against poverty and of sudden and overwhelming success.

When the young poet had completed his high-school course in Dayton, Ohio, in 1891, he could find nothing better to do than to work as an elevator boy at four dollars a week. The first two collections of his verse he was forced to issue privately. *Oak and Ivy*, though dated 1893, really appeared a little before Christmas, 1892; and *Majors and Minors*, dated 1895, was not actually issued until early in the next year. Of this latter work William Dean Howells wrote a full-page review in the issue of *Harper's Weekly* that contained an account of William McKinley's first nomination for the presidency. Dunbar was then launched upon his larger fame, and *Lyrics of Lowly Life*, published by Dodd, Mead & Company in 1896, gave him a hold upon the reading public.

After a visit to England he was given employment as an assistant in the Library of Congress, Washington; but this position he left after fifteen months, as the confinement and the late work at night on his own account were making rapid inroads on his health. Early in 1899 he went South, visiting Tuskegee and other institutions, and giving many readings. Later in the year he went to Colorado in a vain search for health.

Meanwhile books were appearing in rapid succession, novels and short-story collections as well as poems. After *Lyrics of Lowly Life* came *Lyrics of the Hearthside*, *Lyrics of Love and Laughter*, and *Lyrics of Sunshine and Shadow;* and selections from these books were also given in six especially illustrated volumes. The first of the novels, *The Uncalled*, written in London, reflected the poet's thought of entering the ministry. It was followed by *The Love of Landry*, reflecting the sojourn in Colorado, *The Fanatics*, which has a background of the Civil War, and *The Sport of the Gods*, which portrays vividly the life of a Southern family transplanted to New York. Collections of short stories were *Folks from Dixie*, *The Strength of Gideon and Other Stories*, *In Old Plantation Days*, and *The Heart of Happy Hollow*.

Dunbar had not completed his thirty-fourth year when he died, but already he had lived his "millions of years." [1]

[1] For further consideration of Dunbar and his work see Benjamin Brawley, *Paul Laurence Dunbar* (Chapel Hill, 1936), a brief biography by the present author, and *The Best Stories of Paul Laurence Dunbar*, for which he also served as editor (Dodd, Mead & Co., 1938). The original issues of Dunbar's poems are all now out of print, but the volume, *Complete Poems* (Dodd, Mead & Co., 1913), is still accessible. For a general consideration of Dunbar and all the other figures mentioned in this chapter see Benjamin Brawley, *The Negro Genius* (Dodd, Mead & Co., 1937).

180. W. E. Burghardt DuBois.   William Edward Burghardt DuBois was born February 23, 1868, at Great Barrington, Massachusetts. He received the degree of Bachelor of Arts at Fisk University in 1888, the same degree at Harvard in 1890, that of Master of Arts at Harvard in 1891, and, after a season of study at the University of Berlin, the degree of Doctor of Philosophy at Harvard in 1895, his thesis being *The Suppression of the African Slave Trade to the United States of America*. In 1896 he accepted the professorship of History and Economics at Atlanta University, which position he left in 1910 to become the Director of Publicity and Research for the National Association for the Advancement of Colored People. After twenty-four years at this post he returned to Atlanta in 1934, having accepted work in the new Atlanta University.

Dr. DuBois has now issued numerous works, and these are of varied scope. In 1903 fourteen papers, most of which had appeared in *The Atlantic Monthly* and *The World's Work*, were brought together in a volume entitled *The Souls of Black Folk*, whose remarkable style has made it probably the most important book in classic English yet written by a Negro. In 1909 appeared *John Brown*, a contribution to the series of American Crisis Biographies. Two years later was issued a novel, *The Quest of the Silver Fleece*, which has three main themes: the economic position of the Negro agricultural laborer, the subsidizing of certain Negro schools, and life and society in the city of Washington. *Darkwater* (1920), a later collection of essays, was not quite as successful as *The Souls of Black Folk*, the tone being somewhat too strident for the most felicitous effect; nor was *Dark Princess* (1928), another novel, a work to add to the reputation of the author. Very different, however, was *The Gift of Black Folk* (1924), a contribution to a series fostered by the Knights of Columbus largely to offset the propaganda of the Ku Klux Klan. The central chapter undertook to show "how the black fugitive, soldier, and freedman after the Civil War helped to restore the Union, establish public schools, enfranchise the poor white, and initiate industrial democracy in America." This idea was carried further in *Black Reconstruction* (1935), a large work that attempted nothing less than a revision of the conventional view of the period with which it dealt.

In general, Dr. DuBois has helped to give to his people a new sense of literary values and scholarly achievement and, in so doing, he has been an inspiration to a host of younger men.

181. James Weldon Johnson. James Weldon Johnson (1871-1938) had a varied career as teacher, author, and publicist. In 1897, while still living in his home city, Jacksonville, Florida, he was admitted to the bar. There too, while serving as principal of a high school, he began with his brother, the musician, J. Rosamond Johnson, that collaboration in song-writing that was later to prove so successful. In 1900 one wrote the words and the other the music for "Lift Ev'ry Voice and Sing," now widely known as the Negro national anthem. The next year the brothers removed to New York, where they composed many songs for musical-comedy companies. In 1906 Mr. Johnson accepted the post of United States consul to Puerto Cabello in Venezuela. There he remained until 1909, when he was transferred to Corinto, Nicaragua, where he served until 1912. On returning home he entered upon a notable period of service, first as field secretary and then as secretary of the National Association for the Advancement of Colored People. In 1920 he went to Haiti to investigate conditions under the American occupation, and in 1930 became professor of creative literature at Fisk University. His death was the tragic result of an automobile accident at a railroad crossing in Maine.

The publications of this Negro author were numerous and varied. Among the more important were *Fifty Years and Other Poems* (1917); *The Book of American Negro Poetry* (1922), edited with an introduction that made a distinct contribution; *God's Trombones: Seven Negro Sermons in Verse* (1927), in which the author endeavored to catch something of the rhythm and imagery of the older Negro preachers; *Black Manhattan* (1930), which was mainly concerned with giving a record of the Negro's progress on the New York stage; and *Along this Way* (1933), an autobiography.

182. Other Writers, 1900-1920.   Throughout the early years of the century and until his death in 1915, Booker T. Washington remained the outstanding leader of the Negro people in America, and he produced many books reflecting his work. Nothing could surpass *Up from Slavery* (1901), but prominent among his later publications were *My Larger Education* (1911) and *The Man Farthest Down* (1912).

In work of an entirely different sort, distinction was

won by William Stanley Braithwaite, who for some years was known as the foremost critic of current American poetry, irrespective of race. Mr. Braithwaite began publication with two volumes of original poetry, *Lyrics of Life and Love* (1904) and *The House of Falling Leaves* (1908), but entered upon his larger career when he became a regular contributor to the *Boston Evening Transcript* and began the issuing of his annual *Anthology of Magazine Verse*, which appeared each year from 1913 to 1929. The *Transcript* said in an editorial (November 30, 1915): "He has helped poetry to readers as well as to poets. One is guilty of no extravagance in saying that the poets we have—and they may take their place with their peers in any country—and the gathering deference we pay them, are created largely out of the stubborn, self-effacing enthusiasm of this one man."

Alice Dunbar Nelson (1875-1935), who in the earlier years of her career was the wife of Paul Laurence Dunbar, in 1899 produced *The Goodness of St. Rocque, and Other Stories*, a book of quaint charm mainly set in Louisiana. She also wrote a number of excellent poems. Up to 1938 these had not been collected, though one sonnet, "I had not thought of violets of late," was often quoted.

A few years later in her period of greatest activity was Georgia Douglas Johnson, author of three small books of poetry, *The Heart of a Woman* (1918), *Bronze* (1922), and *An Autumn Love Cycle* (1928). Only the second of these is primarily dominated by racial themes.

Meanwhile Dr. Carter G. Woodson had founded in 1916 the *Journal of Negro History* and produced in a very scholarly work, *The Education of the Negro Prior to 1861* (1919), the first of a number of books on the history and education of the Negro.

183. Recent Authors. With the World War came a great change in the temper of Negro literature. Out of the experience of the men who went to France, and those who at home faced the riots of 1919, rose a new consciousness, a new sense of freedom; and writing took on a realistic tone that made the stories and poems of earlier authors seem very far away. A number of young men had anticipated this new temper, and there now appeared several who could speak with force and authority. Only a few of the more prominent authors can be mentioned.

Claude McKay, who came to the United States from Jamaica, was the most vigorous of the new group of poets. A militant sonnet, "If we must die," was much quoted in the months immediately after the war, and the author's best verse was brought together in *Harlem Shadows* (1922). There have since appeared three novels —*Home to Harlem* (1928), *Banjo* (1929), and *Banana Bottom* (1933); also *Gingertown*, a collection of stories.

Langston Hughes, who had a varied experience in travel throughout the world, became the strongest of the writers in free verse. His poem, "The Weary Blues," took first prize in a contest conducted by *Opportunity* in 1925, and the next year became the title-piece in a collection. Among later works are *Not Without Laughter* (1930), a novel set in the Middle West; *The*

Ways of White Folks (1934), stories that use a sharp vein of satire; *Mulatto*, a play that held the stage in New York throughout the winter of 1935-1936; and *The Dream Keeper and Other Poems* (1932), a collection for children containing lyrics of mystery and beauty as well as some in rollicking vein.

Countee Cullen has had more sympathy with tradition and convention than his two compeers just mentioned. In the earlier years of his career he was the recipient of numerous prizes. His works include *Color* (1925), *Copper Sun* (1927), *Caroling Dusk: An Anthology of Verse by Negro Poets* (1927), *The Ballad of the Brown Girl* (1928), *The Black Christ and Other Poems* (1929), *One Way to Heaven*, a novel (1931), and *The Medea and Some Poems* (1935).

Walter White, who for years has served as secretary of the National Association for the Advancement of Colored People, in 1925 produced a novel, *The Fire in the Flint*, that before it closes grips one with a sense of power. It was followed by *Flight* (1926), which was not quite so successful, and by *Rope and Faggot: A Biography of Judge Lynch* (1929).

Jessie Fauset has used material very much like that of Chesnutt, except that she has given this a modern setting. After teaching for some years in the Dunbar High School in Washington, she has served more recently in the DeWitt Clinton High School in New York. Her four novels—*There is Confusion* (1924), *Plum Bun* (1928), *The Chinaberry Tree* (1931), and *Comedy: American Style* (1933)—show steady progress in her chosen medium.

Eric Walrond, who was born in British Guiana and in his youth gained wide acquaintance with the West Indies, came in 1918 to New York. In 1926 he brought forth *Tropic Death*, a collection of ten stories or sketches dealing with the tragedy in the lives of the poorer people in the West Indies. Two or three of these display unusual power.

Rudolph Fisher (1897-1934) was a brilliant figure whose career seemed too soon cut short. Though trained as a physician, he gained literary recognition with two vivid stories of Harlem life that appeared in the *Atlantic*, "The City of Refuge" (February, 1925) and "Blades of Steel" (August, 1927). Two novels were *The Walls of Jericho* (1928) and *The Conjure Man Dies* (1932).

Sterling Brown has written several poems that show a mastery of standard literary forms, such as his noble sonnet "Salutamus," but he has been interested chiefly in the life and idiom of the folk, especially in the songs and ways of the men who move lightly from place to place, as one may see in *Southern Road* (1932).

Zora Neale Hurston has steadily forged forward to prominence in recent years. She has made a specialty of such tales as she heard in her childhood in Florida and as one may hear in a group of men in a railroad or turpentine camp. Her works include *Jonah's Gourd Vine* (1934), a novel; *Mules and Men* (1935), which brings together a number of folk tales and describes voodoo practices in the South; and *Tell My Horse* (1938), which reflects vividly a long sojourn in Haiti.

Arna Bontemps first attracted attention with a poem, "Golgotha Is a Mountain," that took a prize in the

PAUL ROBESON, VERSATILE NEGRO GENIUS—FIRST-RANK
ATHLETE, SINGER, AND ACTOR

Opportunity contest of 1926, and his first sustained effort in fiction was a story of the race track, *God Sends Sunday* (1931); but he has since applied his high literary gift chiefly to themes using an historical background, as one may see from *Black Thunder* (1936), a story based on the attempted insurrection of Gabriel Prosser in Virginia in 1800.

Richard Wright, whose home was in Mississippi, went after a varied experience to New York City; and when *Story Magazine* offered a prize of $500 for the best manuscript submitted by anyone connected with the Federal Writers' Projects, against strong competition he was the winner. His four long stories were brought together in a book entitled *Uncle Tom's Children* (1938), which is unsparing in its realism, but often forceful in its vivid prose.

184. **Drama and the Stage.** For a long time the American public seemed uninterested in the serious portrayal of Negro life; we have noted that, at the middle of the last century, even such a capable performer as Ira Aldridge had to remain in Europe to receive due recognition. Within recent years, however, there has been the beginning of a change; in the decade 1920-1930 Negro themes were used by men not belonging to the race in three highly successful plays—*The Emperor Jones*, by Eugene O'Neill, *In Abraham's Bosom*, by Paul Green, and *The Green Pastures*, adapted by Marc Connelly from Roark Bradford's *Ol' Man Adam and His Chillun*.

No Negro playwright has yet risen to eminence, but

there has lately been much activity, and the one-act plays of Randolph Edmonds are in the right direction.

Four figures on the stage have forced recognition more than most—Charles Gilpin, Richard B. Harrison, Rose McClendon, and Paul Robeson. Gilpin (1872-1930), in his acting in *The Emperor Jones* on the opening night, November 3, 1920, made stage history not only for the Negro but for the country at large. He gave a thrilling performance in a difficult part, and at the close of the season received the vote of the Drama League as one of the ten persons who had contributed most to the American theater in the course of the year. Richard B. Harrison (1864-1935), after long experience as a reader, teacher, and director of amateur theatricals, found at sixty-six years of age, in the chief character in *The Green Pastures*, the role that was to make him famous. With a rare human quality he played for five years without missing a performance, until he was stricken in New York early one afternoon just before time to go on the stage. Rose McClendon (1884-1936), after early experience in dramatics at her church in New York, took a thorough course in her chosen art, and appeared as Goldie, the wife, in *In Abraham's Bosom*, as Serena in *Porgy*, and in numerous other parts; yet, with all that she did, it is doubtful if she ever had a role that gave opportunity for the full play of her talent. Paul Robeson while in college at Rutgers was distinguished in athletics, later he completed a course in law at Columbia, and is perhaps even better known as singer than as actor. He has appeared with great success in the title parts in *The Emperor Jones* and *Othello*, and more recently in various moving pictures. Today he is at home in Russia or France hardly less than in England or the United States.

185. Composers. The foremost name on the roll of Negro composers of music is that of a man whose home was in England but who in so many ways identified himself with the Negro people of the United States that he is often mentioned in connection with them. Samuel Coleridge-Taylor (1875-1912) was born in London, and began the study of the violin when he was six years old. In 1890 he became a student of the Royal Academy of Music. In his third year at this institution he won a prize in composition, and in 1894 was graduated with honor. In 1898 he became famous with his cantata, *Hiawatha's Wedding-Feast*, which was followed by *The Death of Minnehaha* and *Hiawatha's Departure*. The most distinctive work of Coleridge-Taylor, however, is that reflecting his interest in the Negro folk song. All of his works show breadth of treatment, and effects of beauty attained by simple means.

In the United States several composers have won prominence, but only the foremost can be mentioned. Harry T. Burleigh, distinguished also as singer, has shown his technical excellence in such songs as *Jean, One Year* (1914-1915), and *The Young Warrior*, the brilliant war-song the words of which were by James Weldon Johnson. Also of strong quality as *The Grey Wolf*, to words by Arthur Symons, *The Soldier*, a setting of Rupert Brooke's well-known sonnet, and *Ethiopia Saluting the Colors*, to words by Walt Whitman. Mr. Burleigh has made many adaptations of the

Negro melodies, especially for choral work, and he assisted Dvorak in his *New York Symphony* based on the Negro folk songs.

H. Lawrence Freeman, most recently of New York, has produced not less than fourteen operas, though not all of these have received formal presentation. Most notable are *Voodoo, Vendetta,* and *The Octoroon.* Through all of these works passion surges tumultuously, but the composer is always in firm command of his rhythms.

Clarence Cameron White, after study at Howard, spent five years in the Conservatory of Music at Oberlin, and then went to England, where he was associated with Coleridge-Taylor. An earnest teacher, he has included in his career periods of service at Hampton and the West Virginia State College. His numerous pieces for the violin include his *Bandanna Sketches,* also arranged for orchestra and band; and another of his more important productions is a suite, *From the Cotton Fields.* An opera, *Ouanga,* was based on the life of the Haitian liberator, Dessalines, the libretto being by John F. Matheus.

R. Nathaniel Dett received the degree of Bachelor of Music at Oberlin in 1908, and later was honored with the degree of Doctor of Music by both Oberlin and Howard. Studying at Harvard in 1920-1921, he won the Bowdoin essay prize with his paper, "The Emancipation of Negro Music," also the Francis Boott prize in composition. After teaching at two other institutions, he entered in 1913 upon a long period of service at Hampton, remaining until 1931. He has composed several suites for the piano, chiefly *Magnolia, Enchant-ment*, and *In the Bottoms;* his *Danse Juba* has been very popular; and he excels in the writing of anthems. Representative of his later work is the oratorio, *The Order-ing of Moses*, rendered with great success at the Cincinnati Music Festival in May, 1937.

In 1931 the *Afro-American Symphony* of William Grant Still was performed by the Rochester Symphony Orchestra, later being given in Berlin, Stuttgart, and Leipzig; and in general this composer is one from whom much may be expected in the future.

The *Symphony in E Minor* of Florence B. Price, a graduate of the New England Conservatory, was included on a program of the Chicago Symphony Orchestra at the Century of Progress Exposition in 1933. The next year the composer appeared as soloist in her own work at the Chicago Musical College.

On July 3, 1933, a music-drama, *Tom Tom*, by Shirley Graham, was given its first performance in the municipal stadium in Cleveland. The author studied at Oberlin, at Howard, at The Institute of Musical Art in New York, and also in Paris, and for three years was director of music at Morgan College in Baltimore. The production of her work was spectacular, with a full orchestra and five hundred singers and dancers, and with Jules Bledsoe in the leading role.

Prominent in all such effort was the performance in November, 1934, of the *Negro Folk Symphony* of William Levi Dawson by the Philadelphia Orchestra under the direction of Dr. Leopold Stokowski. In both 1930 and 1931 Mr. Dawson took first prize in the

Wanamaker Music Contest, and in the former year the second prize also. In 1931 he went to Tuskegee to organize and direct the School of Music, and two years later his group of one hundred singers was on the program on the opening night of Radio City Music Hall in New York.

186. Vocalists. It was but natural that soprano singers should be most distinguished, and we have observed that even before the Civil War one of the first rank appeared in the person of Elizabeth Taylor Greenfield. About 1880 Madame Marie Selika, a singer of uncommon ability and power, won success on the continent of Europe as well as in England and America. In 1887 Flora Batson entered on the period of her greatest fame. Her voice had a compass of three octaves, from a pure soprano, sweet and full, to the rich, round notes of the baritone register. At a great temperance revival in New York she sang for ninety successive nights with tremendous effect one song, "Six Feet of Earth Make Us All One Size." Three or four years later in point both of birth and period of greatest artistic success came Madame Sissieretta Jones, with whose name the "S'wanee River" is inseparably linked in the public mind. She had a voice of great richness and volume, which was assisted by her superb stage presence.

Early in the present century prominence was attained by Madame E. Azalia Hackley, and she was succeeded by Madame Anita Patti Brown, and Madame Florence Cole Talbert. Within recent years the public has heard Madame Lillian Evanti, who made her debut at Nice in *Lakme;* Caterina Jarboro, who, singing with the Chicago Opera Company at the Hippodrome in the summer of 1933, created a sensation as Aida; and Marian Anderson, a contralto.

Miss Anderson is now one of the outstanding singers of the world. She first won notable success in her home city, Philadelphia, as soloist with the Philharmonic Symphony Orchestra. Later came a concert in Town Hall in New York; and her reputation was greatly enhanced in 1925 when she won against three hundred competitors in a contest conducted by the New York Philharmonic Orchestra, the prize being an appearance as soloist at one of the concerts in the Lewisohn open-air series. Since then she has sung in most of the large cities of Europe and America, winning special favor in critical Stockholm and Vienna The *New York Times* said of her voice after a recital, "It is a contralto of stunning range and volume managed with suppleness and grace."

Of the men, Harry T. Burleigh has served for more than forty years as baritone soloist at St. George's Episcopal Church in New York, and for nearly as long at Temple Emanu-El, the Jewish synagogue on Fifth Avenue. Roland Hayes, a tenor, in the years just after the World War won such success as had never before been achieved by a Negro singer. In Symphony Hall in Boston and Carnegie Hall in New York, he has sung again and again to vast audiences, and in general has reflected credit upon the people whom he represented. Paul Robeson, already mentioned among the actors, has a singing voice that is round and manly, with the quality of extraordinary appeal. He has been singularly successful in concert engagements. Jules Bledsoe has also been both actor and singer. A baritone, he excels in noble or dignified parts. In 1932 he sang the role of Amonasro in *Aida* in a performance by a summer grand opera company in Cleveland, and received an ovation. Later he appeared in various cities in Gruenberg's opera based on *The Emperor Jones*. R. Todd Duncan, of the faculty of the School of Music at Howard, has a fine baritone voice and a deep sense of musical values. He has been increasingly successful within recent years.

187. Instrumentalists. Among the players on different instruments there are now so many capable performers that a full consideration of their work would call for a volume in itself.

For some years Hazel Harrison and Raymond Augustus Lawson have been outstanding among the pianists. Miss Harrison, originally of Chicago, went to Germany for prolonged periods of study, and most recently has been on the faculty at Howard. Her programs feature numbers from Bach and Liszt and regularly leave an impression of masterly achievement. Mr. Lawson has conducted in Hartford one of the leading studios in New England. He has appeared more than once as a soloist with the Hartford Philharmonic Orchestra and on other notable occasions as well.

Among the organists one cannot fail to note Melville Charlton, now of the Religious School of Temple Emanu-El in New York; Roy W. Tibbs, professor of music at Howard; and Orrin Suthern, of Cleveland and Tuskegee, who by all critics is acclaimed as one of the most sensitive of the younger artists.

Among the leading violinists are Louia Vaughn Jones, a teacher at Howard and a brilliant performer, and Gertrude Martin, of New York.

188. Painters. Prominent among the painters of the world for four decades was Henry Ossawa Tanner (1859-1938), who spent his early years in Philadelphia and in 1891 went to Europe for special study. At first his life in Paris was one of pitiless economy, but he persevered and at length succeeded. "Daniel in the Lions' Den" in the Salon of 1896 brought "honorable mention," his first official recognition. Soon afterward he made his first visit to Palestine. "The Resurrection of Lazarus" (1897) was bought by the French Government and now hangs in the Luxembourg. The enthusiasm awakened was so great that a friend wrote to the painter at Venice: "Come home, Tanner, to see the crowds behold your picture." Within the next few years the artist won numerous medals and prizes—at the Paris Exposition in 1900, the Pan-American Exposition in Buffalo in 1901, the Louisiana Purchase Exposition in St. Louis in 1904, and at San Francisco in 1915; also the Walter Lippincott Prize in Philadelphia in 1900, and in 1906 the Harris Prize of five hundred dollars for the best picture in the annual exhibition of American paintings at the Art Institute in Chicago. Among Tanner's later pictures, most of which were on religious subjects, were "The Annunciation," "A Flight into Egypt," and "Christ and Nicodemus."

William Edouard Scott, now best known for his mural and portrait work, was born in Indianapolis in 1884. After some years at the Art Institute in Chicago, where he took various prizes, he went to Paris to continue his studies. There he encountered difficulties innumerable, but at last, in 1912, saw one of his paintings, "La Pauvre Voisine," accepted at the Salon. The Argentine Government later purchased the picture for six hundred dollars. Among the numerous murals on which the artist has worked in more recent years are those in a bank in Edwardsville, Illinois, the City Hospital in Indianapolis, the State House in Springfield, Illinois, and the Court House in Fort Wayne, Indiana. In 1931, under the auspices of the Rosenwald Foundation, Mr. Scott studied Negro types in Haiti.

In no field of Negro life has development been more rapid since the World War than in that of the fine arts. With the new day came not only freedom but also more attention to racial subjects. A catalogue issued by the Harmon Foundation in 1935 gives sketches of a hundred and nine painters or sculptors, with brief mention of several more; and one might note that with the work of such men as Albert I. Cassell, of Washington, Paul R. Williams, of Los Angeles, and Hilyard R. Robinson, of Washington, there has been a notable advance in architecture. Especially well organized is the studio in New York founded and directed by Augusta Savage, in which, in 1935, there were as many as forty-six students.

Much has been done by earnest teachers, most of whom are themselves rising artists. At Howard University the director, in many ways a pioneer, is Professor James V. Herring; and associated with him are Lois Mailou Jones, James A. Porter, and James Lesesne Wells,

all of whom have exhibited frequently. At the Cheyney
State Teachers College is Laura Wheeler Waring, who
has studied both at home and abroad, and has illustrated
books for some of the leading publishers in the country.
To Atlanta University went in 1931 Hale A. Woodruff,
who is especially interested in murals. Elton Clay Fax,
who received his degree at Syracuse and completed four
murals for the Dunbar Junior High School in Baltimore,
is now at Claflin University; and Allan Freelon, who
was graduated at the University of Pennsylvania and for
four years held a scholarship at the Pennsylvania
Museum of Art, is an assistant director in the public
schools of Philadelphia.

One does not go far in a study of the painters (or
the sculptors) of recent years before he is conscious of
a cleavage between those who are in line with tradition
and those who may be said to work in a modernistic
vein. Prominent in the first group would be the late
Edwin A. Harleston, who excelled in portrait work;
William McKnight Farrow, of the Art Institute in Chicago; Palmer C. Hayden, who excels in the treatment
of marine subjects; and Laura Wheeler Waring. Outstanding among the modernists are Archibald J. Motley,
Jr., and Aaron Douglas. Mr. Motley studied at the Art
Institute of Chicago and abroad, and as early as 1928
gave at the New Galleries in New York the first one-
man show by any Negro artist since that of Tanner,
practically all the paintings being sold to collectors. He
has taken part in numerous exhibitions and has won the
Eisendrath Prize of the American-Scandinavian Foundation in Stockholm. Mr. Douglas, a graduate of the

University of Nebraska, studied in New York and Paris, then taught for two years in Kansas City. He has contributed drawings and designs to numerous magazines and illustrated several books, but his chief work is in murals. He made the decorations for the Fisk University Library, the Sherman Hotel in Chicago, the 135th Street Branch of the Public Library of New York, the 135th Street Branch of the Young Men's Christian Association in New York, and the Hall of Negro Life at the Texas Centennial Exposition in Dallas.[2]

189. Sculptors. Outstanding among the sculptors in the first two decades of the century, and indeed almost a lonely figure, was Meta Vaux Warrick, who first compelled recognition of her talent by her work at the Pennsylvania School of Industrial Art, which she attended for four years. At her graduation in 1898 she won a prize for metal work by a crucifix upon which hung the figure of Christ torn by anguish, and, in a postgraduate year, the George K. Crozier first prize for the best work in modeling throughout the year. She then went to Paris, where she met St. Gaudens and other artists. At last came a day when the great Rodin himself, thrilled by the figure in "Silent Sorrow," beamed upon her with the attitude of a father and said, "Mademoiselle, you are a sculptor; you have the sense of form." "The Wretched," a remarkable piece of work with seven

[2] For further consideration of the artists mentioned see Brawley, *The Negro Genius*, and Alain Locke, *Negro Art, Past and Present* (Washington: Associates in Negro Folk Education, 1937), which emphasizes the modernistic temper. A definitive work in the whole field by James A. Porter, himself one of the artists, is yet to be published.

figures representing as many forms of anguish, was exhibited in the Salon in 1903; and along with it went "The Impenitent Thief." Another production of these years was "Man Carrying Dead Body," in which a soldier bore upon his back the body of a comrade that had lain on the field for days. More and more the artist became known as one who excelled in the portrayal of the tragic and horrible. In 1907 she was called on by the officials of the Jamestown Tercentennial Exposition for a series of tableaux representing the advance of the Negro, and in 1913 for a group for the New York State Emancipation Proclamation Commission. Meanwhile, in 1909, she had become the wife of Dr. Solomon C. Fuller, of Framingham, Massachusetts. In more recent years she has shown a strong social note, as in "Exodus," which includes several figures representing Negroes leaving the South for the North at the time of the World War. Mrs. Fuller was one of the first women invited to join the Boston Art Club. She has served as a judge in numerous contests, and in general has been an inspiration to younger artists.

Since the World War the same general influences have been at work in sculpture as in painting. There has been more freedom, also a strong tendency toward modernism. Prominent both as teacher and artist is Nancy Elizabeth Prophet, a graduate of the Rhode Island School of Design, now of Atlanta University, whose sculpture has appeared in numerous exhibits both at home and abroad. Richmond Barthé, who was born in Mississippi in 1901, studied for four years at the Art Institute of Chicago and later in New York. He exhibited at the Century of Progress Exposition in Chicago and at the Texas Centennial in Dallas, and otherwise has had wide recognition. Recently he has been at work on two forty-foot panels for the Federal Government. These are to be in relief, in stone, and are to be used for the retaining walls of an amphitheatre on the Harlem River Housing Project. The subjects were suggested by the scenes of the dance and the exodus in *The Green Pastures*. Sargent Johnson, born in Boston in 1888, spent his early years in Virginia, and it was not until after his marriage that he was able to attend the California School of Fine Arts. There he learned to work in several media but proved to be most interested in sculpture. His productions show unusual technical excellence, without unnecessary detail. Mr. Johnson has taken several prizes in the course of his career and in 1934 was elected to the Council Board of the San Francisco Art Association.

CHAPTER XVIII

THE NEGRO IN AMERICAN LIFE

190. Periods of Negro History. It is probably clear from the preceding pages that the history of the Negro people in the United States falls into certain well-defined periods.

First of all there was the colonial era, extending from 1619, when the first Negroes came to Jamestown, to 1776, the date which formally signalized the opening of the Revolutionary War. This divides into two parts, with a line coming at the year 1705. Before this date the status of the Negro was more or less undefined; the system of servitude was only gradually passing into the sterner one of slavery, and especially in the middle colonies there was considerable intermixture of the races. By 1705, however, slave codes were taking on some degree of uniformity; and, while the next seventy years witnessed increasing numbers, they saw no racial coherence or spiritual outlook, only a spasmodic insurrection here and there indicating the yearning for a better day.

With the Revolution came a change. The second period extends from this war to the Civil War, and is also divided into two parts, with a line at the year 1830. In the decades immediately succeeding the Revolution was put forth the first effort toward formal organization, represented by the work of such men as Richard Allen and Prince Hall; but, in spite of a quickening racial consciousness, most of the Negro people remained in the same situation as before, and the invention of the cotton gin led to the development of great plantations. About the year 1830, however, the very hatred and ignominy visited upon the Negro indicated at least that he was beginning to rise in status. Lynching increased, burlesque on the stage tended to depreciate the race, and the South became united as never before in its defense of slavery. At the same time the Abolitionists challenged the attitude that was becoming popular; the Negroes themselves became more articulate; and Nat Turner's insurrection thrust baldly before the American people the great moral and economic problem with which they had to deal.

The third period extends from the Civil War to the opening of the World War. Like the others it falls into two parts, the division coming at the year 1895. The thirty years from 1865 to 1895 may be regarded as an era in which the race, now emancipated, was mainly under the dominance of political ideals. Several men went to Congress and popular education began to be emphasized; but the difficulties of Reconstruction and the activities of the Ku Klux Klan were succeeded by peonage, and in the South disfranchisement at length was accepted as the solution of the political phase of the problem. The twenty years from 1895 to 1915 formed a period of unrest and violence, but also of solid economic and social progress under the dominant influence of Booker T. Washington.

With the World War the Negro people came face to face with new and vast problems of economic adjustment, and passed into a fourth and entirely different period of their racial history in America.

191. The Negro's Influence on American History. That is not all. The most casual glance at any such account as we have given will emphasize the prominence of the Negro in the general history of the United States. Other races have come, sometimes in large numbers or with great gifts, but it is upon this race that the country's history has turned as on a pivot. In the colonial era it was the economic advantage of slavery over servitude that caused it to displace that institution as a system of labor. In the preliminary draft of the Declaration of Independence a noteworthy passage arraigned the king of England for his insistence upon the slave trade, though this section was later suppressed for reasons of policy. The war itself revealed clearly the fallacy of the position of the patriots, who fought for their rights as Englishmen but not for the fundamental rights of man; and their attitude received formal expression in the compromises that entered into the making of the Constitution. The expansion of the Southwest depended on the labor of the Negro, and the question of fugitives was a prominent factor in the Seminole Wars. The long struggle culminating in the Civil War was mainly concerned with the status of the Negro in the republic, and the legislation after that contest determined for a generation the history not only of the South but very largely of the nation as well. The later disfranchising acts have had overwhelming importance, the unequal system of national representation controlling the election of 1916 and thus the attitude of America in the World War.

192. The Problem of Racial Prejudice. All this is obvious; even so, it is still sometimes maintained that the Negro is the one race that cannot and will not be permitted to enter into the full promise of American life. Other elements, it is said, even if difficult to assimilate, may gradually be brought into the body politic, but the Negro is the one element that may be tolerated and utilized but not fully absorbed.

When one asks the reason for this attitude, reference is sometimes made to grave social crimes; but statistics have repeatedly shown that this contention will not hold, and that lynchings have sometimes taken place after minor offences or even by mistake. The more one studies the matter, the more he realizes that any feeling there may be against the Negro finds its ultimate origin in the prejudice that races or groups of people have toward those who are superficially different from themselves, though of course there may be some basis in questions of labor or in fear as to self- or racial preservation. Even if the Negro did not have to work at all, and if the race did not include a single criminal, in American opinion there would still be a question.

We are thus led to ask: Just what is the race worth as a constructive factor in American civilization? Is it finally to be an agency for the upbuilding of the nation or simply one of the forces that retard? What is its real promise in American life?

193. The Negro's Contribution. In answer to this the Negro points to his record in labor, to that as a soldier, and to his contribution to art.

The South—and to some extent the whole country—depends upon Negro men and women as the stable labor supply in such occupations as farming, mining, cooking, and washing. Not less than 50 per cent of the total number of Negro men at work are engaged in raising farm products either on their own account or by way of assisting somebody else; and if along with the farmers we take those engaged in the building and hand trades, in saw and planing mills, and those employed as railway firemen and porters, draymen, teamsters, and coal-mine operators, we shall have a total of not less than 70 per cent engaged in such work as represents the very foundation of American industry. Of the women nearly 80 per cent are engaged as farm laborers, cooks, or washerwomen, so that they do much of the hardest and at the same time much of the most necessary work in our home and industrial life. When the war came and the men were summoned to France, upon the women fell not only the brunt of heavy agricultural labor in the South but also much of the work in the great industrial plants in the North. Meanwhile the Negro stevedore became famous for his contribution to the success of the Allied forces.

Then there is the Negro soldier. In all our history there are no pages more heroic, more thrilling, more pathetic, than those detailing the exploits of black men. We recall the deeds at Port Hudson, Fort Pillow, and Fort Wagner. Remember, at Santiago and San Juan Hill, not only how Negro men went gallantly to the charge but also how the men of a black regiment faced pestilence that the ranks of their white comrades might not be decimated. Again and again has the Negro been summoned to the colors, in the World War summoned out of all proportion to his numbers; and in peace or war, in victory or danger, he has ever been loyal to the Stars and Stripes.

Finally there is the Negro's aesthetic gift. It is possible for him to achieve eminence in science, education, or religion just as any other man may, and sometimes he has done so; but the fact remains that, so far, distinction won by members of the race in America has been most frequently in some one of the arts. We might refer to the oratory of Douglass, to the poetry of Dunbar, to the paintings of Tanner, to the tragic sculpture of Meta Warrick Fuller, and to a long line of singers and musicians. After the World War the Negro, long neglected, became prominent as a subject for artistic treatment. Of the plays that were most popular on the New York stage in the decade 1920-30, not less than three —*The Emperor Jones, In Abraham's Bosom,* and *The Green Pastures*—were on Negro themes. Perhaps even greater has been the influence in sculpture. To modern plastic art Negro sculpture has made two contributions that must inevitably go on working: (1) its way of building up a design from the dissociated parts of a natural object and (2) the array of actual designs it has achieved by this method. The artist is now free from the Renaissance tradition. "In an age when more than one voice has been heard to say that sculpture is obsolete, and the plastic arts exhausted, Negro art has brought creative forces that may prove to be inexhaustible." [1]

194. Proscription and Segregation. Such gifts and contributions as have been mentioned are now well known, and are acknowledged by the American people in increasing measure; at the same time they merely modify rather than wholly do away with the feeling that has been suggested.

This is the situation in spite of the fact that the Negro people, now a tenth of the nation's population, have for the last century been increasing in number only about half as fast as the white people, inasmuch as comparatively few have entered the country from abroad. To their lot it has fallen to have throughout the South and to some extent elsewhere separate, and hence in most cases inferior, schools, traveling facilities, and civic advantages.

Especially notable within the last three decades have been the laws having to do with residential segregation. Beginning about 1910 a wave of these laws swept over the country. Within a year such cities as Baltimore, Dallas, Asheville, Richmond, St. Louis, and Louisville passed such ordinances, and there were many stern contests. A case from Louisville was taken to the Supreme Court of the United States, and that tribunal decreed that the enactment found no justification in the national Constitution. In direct violation of this opinion, however, the Supreme Court of Louisiana, on March 2, 1925,

[1] Paul Guillaume and Thomas Munro, *Primitive Negro Sculpture* (New York: Harcourt, Brace & Co., 1926), p. 134.

approved a segregation ordinance in New Orleans that provided for the written consent of those of the race in the majority, in a given block, as condition of the residence there by a member of another race. This enactment was also taken to the United States Supreme Court, and that body simply referred to the Louisville decision. Since then segregation has generally taken the form of special agreements among property owners.

Extraordinary attention was attracted to the case of Dr. Ossian H. Sweet, a physician in Detroit, who, on September 8, 1924, in the face of threats, moved into a new home with his wife and baby. His brother, Henry, a dentist, and eight other friends helped him to garrison the house. On the night of September 9 a mob stoned the home, and by fire from within a white man was shot and killed. All within the building were then arrested and charged with conspiracy to commit first degree murder. A trial of all the defendants resulted in disagreement on the part of the jury. The defendants then chose to stand trial separately, Henry Sweet being placed first. The National Association for the Advancement of Colored People became interested; Clarence Darrow became the chief counsel; and an acquittal was at last secured. Early in 1928 the other cases were dismissed.

195. Racial Aspiration. Significant in the face of such events is the new attitude of the Negro.

For some decades after the Civil War, when conditions were uncertain and ignorance was rampant, the black man had not developed pride in his race, and he sometimes went afar for his ideals.

Today, however, there are signs of change. In almost

every city there are beautiful homes owned by Negroes. Some men have won high attainment in scholarship, and the promise daily grows brighter in art and science. Accordingly, the Negro now loves his own; he teaches his boy about black heroes; and he honors the womanhood of the race as never before. Meanwhile various co-operative enterprises testify to the new racial self-respect. A people has been reborn; a whole race has found its soul.

Thus it is that fourteen million Americans of darker hue now look forward to all that is best in the life of the republic. They are not satisfied with anything less than the full status of citizens. In the words of Senator Foraker on the soldiers at Brownsville, "They ask no favors because they are Negroes, but only justice because they are men."

196. The Negro and American Citizenship. It is obvious of course that this position is the only one that can accord with the American theory of government. The republic was founded as a genuine democracy. Says the Declaration of Independence: "We hold these truths to be self-evident: That all men are created equal; that they are endowed by their Creator with certain inalienable rights; that among these are life, liberty, and the pursuit of happiness." The Fifteenth Amendment to the Constitution says: "The right of citizens of the United States to vote shall not be denied or abridged by the United States or by any State on account of race, color, or previous condition of servitude." These statements have been fiercely assailed; but their meaning is clear, and they have been reinforced by more than one decision of the United States Supreme Court. They emphasize the fact that in this country there can be no permanently submerged or underprivileged group.

197. The World Aspect of the Negro Problem. The question at issue, however, is today larger than any one race or nation. There are two fundamental assumptions upon which all so-called Western civilization has been based, that of racial and that of religious superiority; and a popular English poet has sung of "the white man's burden" and of "lesser breeds without the law." Such an attitude shows no respect for another people's tradition, and the whole world is now rising as never before against the selfishness of the great powers. Today large portions of Asia and Africa are in turmoil; and, in spite of protestations of goodwill, much of South America views with suspicion the great country at the North.

As to the Negro, one can but recall the words of Marcus Garvey at Madison Square Garden in New York in 1924: "From our distinct racial-group idealism we feel that no black man is good enough to govern the white man, and no white man good enough to rule the black man; and so of all races and peoples. . . . As far as humanity goes, all men are equal, and especially where peoples are intelligent enough to know what they want. At this time all peoples know what they want; it is liberty. Let no black man feel that he has the exclusive right to the world and other men none, and let no white man feel that way either. The world is the property of all mankind, and each and every group is entitled to a portion. The black man now wants his, and in terms uncompromising he is asking for it."

198. The Obligation and Duty of the Citizen. This insistence on what a people wants, however, is only part of the answer to their problem. A race, like an individual, has not only rights but obligations, not only privileges but duties; and in the last analysis the strongest basis for advancement is character. Booker T. Washington well said, "Freedom can never be given; it must be purchased." That means that if one wants the rights of citizenship, he must *deserve* the rights of citizenship, and live down any point that may be made against him.

No man who loafs and drinks, for instance, and whose family has to be supported by public funds, can expect to have the full honor and integrity of a citizen; the burden rests upon him to make himself a constructive factor in the upbuilding of his city and state.

As to the matter of residence in certain areas of which we have spoken, the point has been made that whenever Negroes move into a community in considerable numbers, property values decline. That is a fact with which we have to reckon. Homes crowded with lodgers, yards covered with trash, radios that are too loud or that play at too late hours—all such things as these make many people feel that they would not care to live in a given neighborhood; and when many want to leave, any property there becomes less desirable to a purchaser. In no way can young Negro Americans better improve the whole situation relating to their people than by making it a point to keep their yards and streets as clean as possible, and to do nothing that would make life unpleasant for a neighbor. When millions of Negroes are determined to give only of their best to the country and to leave off everything that might detract, their general estate will be infinitely higher.

199. The Ultimate Issue. Finally, one may note that in the last analysis the leadership of the world is not a matter of race, or even of professed religion, but of principle.

Other countries have failed, and to the United States has come that moral leadership, that obligation to do the right thing, that opportunity to exhibit the highest honor in all affairs foreign or domestic, which is the true test of greatness. The Negro is but one of the problems with which the nation has to deal, and in the handling of this and of all other problems the United States is the hope of the world.

Into its civilization have entered not one but many races. All go forth against a common enemy; all must share alike the duties of citizenship. In such a land the law can know no difference of race or class or creed, provided that all are devoted to the general welfare. Such is the obligation resting today upon our country —a challenge to find democratic ways of solving economic, social, and moral questions such as never before faced the children of men. That it might be worthy of its opportunity all would hope; to the fulfilment of its destiny all should help. The eyes of the world are upon it; the scepter of the ages is in its hand.

QUESTIONS FOR REVIEW

For answers see the table of contents and the index; also consult other books on the history and life of the Negro, especially the latest edition of the *Negro Year Book*, edited by M. N. Work. In some cases the large encyclopedias and the more general works on American history will also be valuable.

1. What is the origin of the word *Negro?*
2. From what part of the African coast were most slaves brought to this country?
3. What was the special provision affecting slavery (the Asiento Contract) in the Peace of Utrecht?
4. Distinguish between servitude, or indenture, and slavery.
5. Which were the first colonies or states that undertook to put an end to slavery?
6. How did slavery affect the making of the Constitution of the United States?
7. In what large way did Toussaint L'Ouverture affect the history of the United States?
8. Describe the actual means of securing slaves on the African coast.
9. Why was it that the slave trade was regarded as worse than slavery itself? (Find and read Whittier's poem "The Slave Ships.")
10. Who were some of the men who in England worked most earnestly for Negro emancipation? (In

addition to those mentioned in the text, look up in an encyclopedia Zachary Macaulay, Henry Brougham, and John Bright.)

11. Tell exactly what was done for freedom by each of the following: William Lloyd Garrison, Elijah P. Lovejoy, Charles Sumner.

12. What was the argument by which the South defended slavery, and wherein was this fallacious?

13. What did the Negro have to do with the outbreak of the Seminole Wars?

14. What men would you regard as the foremost Negro insurrectionists? Compare them.

15. Just when did the first American Negroes go to Liberia, and when did that country become a republic?

16. In what notable case did John Quincy Adams appear before the United States Supreme Court in behalf of a group of Negroes?

17. What was the issue raised in Boston by Anthony Burns?

18. Why was the Dred Scott Decision regarded as important?

19. Name eight Negroes who were prominent in the life of their people before 1860.

20. Who were some of the Northern men who led Negro soldiers in the Civil War?

21. Who said, "Colonel, I will bring back these colors to you on honor, or report to God the reason why"? Who said, "Boys, the old flag never touched the ground"?

22. What good did the Freedmen's Bureau do? On the other hand, what is to be said against it?

23. Macaulay in his essay on Milton says that if a man is to learn to swim, he must first get into the water. Apply this statement to the problem of giving the Negro the ballot immediately after the Civil War.

24. From what sources do the following institutions receive their main support: Howard, Hampton, Virginia Union, Clark, Talladega, Xavier?

25. In what large way did Henry W. Grady affect the history of the Negro?

26. What is meant by the "grandfather clause" in some state constitutions?

27. What is the situation that leads some people to say today that the vote of one white man in South Carolina or Mississippi is equal to that of eight or ten white men in Kansas or Massachusetts?

28. Name six Negro men who have had seats in the Congress of the United States, telling what states they represented.

29. What are land-grant colleges? Name six of them and tell where they are located.

30. What is peonage? Do you know of any sections of the United States where it is practiced today?

31. Quote four striking sentences from Booker T. Washington.

32. In what large ways have the wars in which the United States has engaged affected the life of the Negro in this country?

33. What in the history of the Negro is the significance of Fort Wagner, Brownsville, Carrizal, Houston, East St. Louis?

34. What was the record of the Negro soldier in the American Army during the World War?

35. For some years immediately after the World War, Marcus Garvey made a strong appeal to many Negroes in the United States: why was this?

36. State the purpose of each of the following organizations: the National Negro Business League, the National Association for the Advancement of Colored People, the National Urban League.

37. What notable decisions affecting the Negro have been made in recent years by the United States Supreme Court?

38. Who said, "They ask no favors because they are Negroes, but only justice because they are men"?

39. What are the chief business enterprises operated by the Negro in the United States today?

40. At what periods in his history has the American Negro made the greatest migration from the South to the North or West?

41. What is the Spingarn Medal? Name five persons to whom it has been given.

42. For each of the following fields name three Negroes who have made highly distinctive contributions: the church, medicine, invention, the stage, painting, sculpture.

43. Name at least four Negro authors who flourished before the World War and indicate the line of their achievement. Name four who have come into prominence since the World War.

44. With what organization is A. Philip Randolph connected? What is the significance of his achievement?

45. How did the Negro fare in connection with some of the special agencies set up by the Federal Government in the administrations of President Franklin D. Roosevelt?

46. How does the percentage of Negro population in the United States today compare with what it was in 1790? How do you account for the difference?

47. How does the number of lynchings for the last five years compare with that for the period 1890-1895?

48. Wendell Phillips believed fully in democracy; Jefferson Davis did not. State some of the opposing arguments and apply these to the Negro.

49. A few years ago considerable discussion was awakened when someone gave a list of the ten Negroes in American history who were said to have made the most outstanding contribution to the life of their people and their country. Give your own list of ten.

50. Show as well as you can how the problems and aspirations of the Negro people in the United States are related to those of other struggling people throughout the world.

SELECTED BIBLIOGRAPHY

The list of books that follows is necessarily brief. The more advanced student will naturally wish to consult Work, Monroe N. *A Bibliography of the Negro in Africa and America.* New York: H. W. Wilson Co., 1929; perhaps also the author's *The Negro Genius* (for literary characters) and *Negro Builders and Heroes* (for special subjects in biography); Locke, Alain *The New Negro;* Johnson, Charles S. *The Negro in American Civilization;* and Gallagher, Buell G. *American Caste and the Negro College.* While there has been much interest in the study of the Negro within recent years, comparatively few books strictly in the field of history have been produced; accordingly the periodical literature is of increasing importance.

Collections or Series

Annual reports of the General Education Board and other organizations interested in the education of the Negro

Atlanta University Studies of Negro Problems

Files of the *Crisis* and *Opportunity*, New York, the *Journal of Negro History* and the *Journal of Negro Education*, Washington, D. C., and the *Virginia Magazine of History*

Johns Hopkins University Studies in Historical and Political Science

Laws of the State of North Carolina, compiled by Henry Potter, J. L. Taylor, and Bart. Yancey. Raleigh, 1821

Occasional papers of the American Negro Academy (now discontinued), especially No. 7, *Right on the Scaffold, or the Martyrs of 1822*, by A. H. Grimké, and No. 11, *The Negro and the Elective Franchise*

Statutes at Large, being a collection of all the laws of Virginia from the first session of the Legislature, in the year 1619, by William Waller Hening. Richmond, 1819-20

The Statutes at Large of South Carolina, edited by Thomas Cooper. Columbia, S. C., 1837

Individual Works

As has been suggested, even a sharply curtailed bibliography for Chapter XVII alone would carry us far beyond the space for the present list; hence, for subjects in literature, music, and art no attempt is here made to duplicate the list in the author's *The Negro Genius.* If with three or four of the more prominent authors there appear to be some exceptions, the reasons will be obvious.

BALLAGH, JAMES CURTIS *A History of Slavery in Virginia*, extra volume XXIV of Johns Hopkins Studies. Baltimore: Johns Hopkins Press, 1902

BASSETT, JOHN SPENCER *Anti-Slavery Leaders of North Carolina*, Series XVI, No. 6, Johns Hopkins Studies. Baltimore: Johns Hopkins Press, 1896

BLAKE, W. O. *The History of Slavery and the Slave Trade.* Columbus, O., 1861

BRAWLEY, BENJAMIN *A Social History of the American Negro* (now out of print). New York: The Macmillan Company, 1921

  Early Negro American Writers (edited). Chapel Hill: The University of North Carolina Press, 1935

  Paul Laurence Dunbar. Chapel Hill: The University of North Carolina Press, 1936

  The Negro Genius (superseding *The Negro in Literature and Art*). New York: Dodd, Mead & Co., 1937

  Negro Builders and Heroes. Chapel Hill: The University of North Carolina Press, 1937

BROOKS, WALTER H. *The Silver Bluff Church.* Washington, 1910

CROMWELL, JOHN W. *The Negro in American History*. Washington, D. C.: The American Negro Academy, 1914

CUTLER, JAMES E. *Lynch Law*, An Investigation into the History of Lynching in the United States. New York: Longmans, Green & Co., 1905

DAVIS, JOHN W. *Land-Grant Colleges for Negroes*, in Publications of West Virginia State College. Institute, W. Va., 1934

DELANY, MARTIN R. *The Condition, Elevation, Emigration, and Destiny of the Colored People of the United States, Politically Considered*. Philadelphia, 1852

DOUGLASS, FREDERICK *My Bondage and My Freedom*. New York, 1855

DuBois, WILLIAM EDWARD BURGHARDT *Suppression of the African Slave Trade*. Cambridge: Harvard University Press, 1896
The Souls of Black Folk (essays and sketches). Chicago: A. C. McClurg & Co., 1903
Darkwater: Voices from within the Veil. New York: Harcourt, Brace & Co., 1920
The Gift of Black Folk. Boston: The Stratford Company, 1924
Black Reconstruction. New York: Harcourt, Brace & Co., 1935

DUNBAR, PAUL LAURENCE *Complete Poems*. New York: Dodd, Mead & Co., 1913
The Best Stories of Paul Laurence Dunbar, selected and edited with an introduction by Benjamin Brawley. New York: Dodd, Mead & Co., 1938

FAUSET, ARTHUR HUFF *Sojourner Truth*. Chapel Hill: The University of North Carolina Press, 1938

FAUST, ALBERT BERNHARDT *The German Element in the United States*. Boston: Houghton Mifflin Company, 1909

FISHER, MILES MARK *A Short History of the Baptist Denomination.* Nashville: Sunday School Publishing Board, 1933

FLEMING, WALTER L. *Documentary History of Reconstruction.* Cleveland: The Arthur H. Clark Co., 1907

GALLAGHER, BUELL G. *American Caste and the Negro College,* with a foreword by William H. Kilpatrick. New York: Columbia University Press, 1938

HART, ALBERT BUSHNELL *Slavery and Abolition,* American Nation Series, XVI. New York: Harper & Bros., 1906
Negro Suffrage (a contribution to the *Boston Evening Transcript* of March 24, 1906, reprinted as a pamphlet by the Niagara Movement)

HELPER, HINTON ROWAN *The Impending Crisis of the South: How to Meet It.* New York, 1857

HIGGINSON, THOMAS WENTWORTH *Army Life in a Black Regiment.* Boston, 1870

HOLMES, DWIGHT OLIVER WENDELL *The Evolution of the Negro College.* New York: Bureau of Publications, Teachers College, Columbia University, 1934

JOHNSON, CHARLES S. *The Negro in American Civilization.* New York: Henry Holt & Co., 1930
The Negro College Graduate. Chapel Hill: The University of North Carolina Press, 1938

JOHNSON, JAMES WELDON *The Book of American Negro Poetry (edited).* New York: Harcourt, Brace & Co., 1922; revised edition, 1931
Black Manhattan. New York: Alfred A. Knopf, Inc., 1930
Along this Way (autobiography). New York: The Viking Press, 1933

LOCKE, ALAIN *The New Negro* (edited). New York, 1925
Negro Art: Past and Present, Bronze Booklets. Washington: Associates in Negro Folk Education, 1937

LOGGINS, VERNON *The Negro Author: His Development in America.* New York: Columbia University Press, 1931

McMaster, John Bach *A History of the People of the United States, from the Revolution to the Civil War*. 8 vols. New York: D. Appleton & Co., 1883-1913

Merriam, George S. *The Negro and the Nation*. New York: Henry Holt & Co., 1906

Moton, Robert Russa *Finding a Way Out* (autobiography). Garden City, N. Y.: Doubleday, Page & Co., 1920

What the Negro Thinks. Garden City, N. Y.: Doubleday, Doran & Co., Inc., 1929

Negro Year Book, edited by Monroe N. Work, 1937-1938. Tuskegee Institute, Ala.: Negro Year Book Publishing Co., 1937

Nell, William C. *The Colored Patriots of the American Revolution*. Boston, 1855

Northup, Solomon *Twelve Years a Slave*. Auburn, Buffalo, London, 1853

Ovington, Mary White *Portraits in Color*. New York: The Viking Press, 1927

Spears, J. R. *The American Slave Trade: An Account of Its Origin, Growth, and Suppression*. New York: Charles Scribner's Sons, 1900

Trotter, James M. *Music and Some Highly Musical People*. Boston, 1878

Washington, Booker T. *Up from Slavery: An Autobiography*. New York: Doubleday, Page & Co., 1900

The Story of the Negro. New York: Doubleday, Page & Co., 1909

My Larger Education. New York: Doubleday, Page & Co., 1911

Selected Speeches, edited by E. Davidson Washington. Garden City, N. Y., 1932

Williams, Charles H. *Sidelights on Negro Soldiers*, with an Introduction by Benjamin Brawley. Boston: B. J. Brimmer Co., 1923

WILLIAMS, GEORGE W. *History of the Negro Race in America from 1619 to 1880.* New York: G. P. Putnam's Sons, 1883

A History of Negro Troops in the War of the Rebellion. New York: Harper & Bros., 1888

WOODSON, CARTER G. *The Education of the Negro Prior to 1861.* New York: G. P. Putnam's Sons, 1915

The History of the Negro Church. Washington: The Associated Publishers, 1921

The Negro in Our History. Sixth Edition. Washington: The Associated Publishers, 1931

Negro Orators and Their Orations (edited). Washington: The Associated Publishers, 1926

WRIGHT, RICHARD R. *Negro Companions of the Spanish Explorers,* pamphlet reprinted from the *American Anthropologist,* Vol. 4, April-June, 1902

INDEX